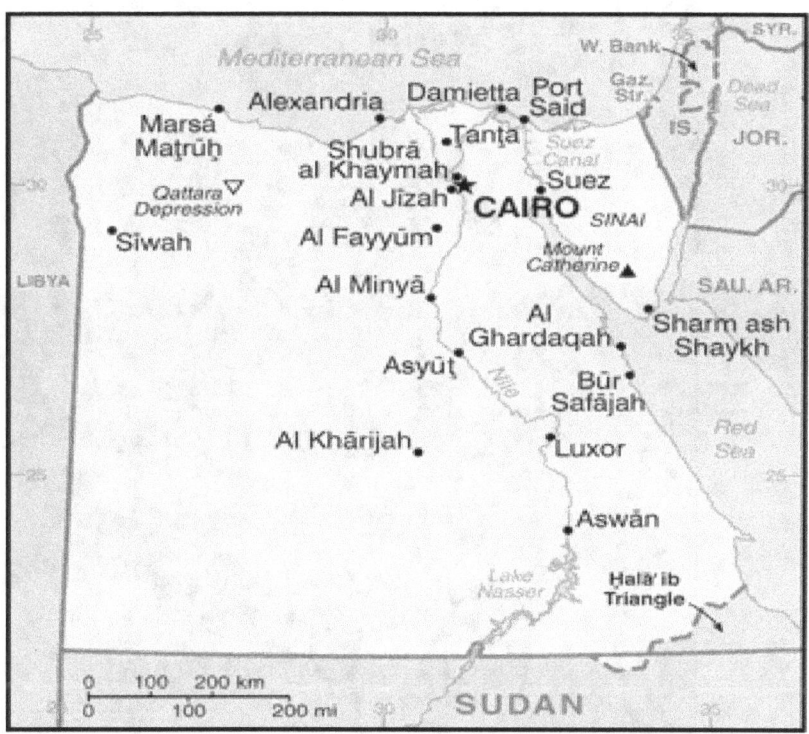

Central Intelligence Agency, 2009
https://www.cia.gov/library/publications/the-world-factbook/index.html

Middle East

Central Intelligence Agency, 2009
https://www.cia.gov/library/publications/the-world-factbook/index.html

Il Binait Dol

Egypt's Hidden Shame

GWENLLIAN MEREDITH

Middle East Connections Consultancy Publications

Massachusetts USA, 2013

Published in the United States by Middle East Connections Consultancy Books

Visit our website at www.Middleeastconnex.com and our blog at http://middleeastconx.blogspot.com/

A Middle East Connections Consultancy Publication

Printed in the United States of America

First Printing July 2013

Amazon Kindle ebooks

Search words: 1. Egypt. 2. Egyptian politics. 3. Egyptian law. 4. Social Science – Gender Issues. 5. Family and Family Relationships. 6. Egyptian education. 7. Social Science – general.

Book cover designed by Gwenllian Meredith. Editing and proofreading by Lynn Kordus. Logo Design by Stormi Knight Graphic Designs, Boston, Massachusetts USA. Please note this book follows the British style.

Printed in the United States of America

PHOTO CREDITS

Gwenn Meredith–photos taken by the author, from the author's personal collection

Photo of Hanna and Souhail Hosni provided by Hanna Hartmann-Hosni

To Troy, Kristine, Austin, Matthew, Trent,

Rhys, Lynn,

and to Hanna & Souhail

TABLE OF CONTENTS

Prologue

Il Binait Dol[1], Egypt's Secret Shame is about the most silent and vulnerable segment of Egyptian society, that of the country's street girls, girls destined to live in vile conditions, without family, virtually alone in the world. An objective of this book is to reveal the shame perpetrated on Egypt's homeless, helpless, and starving girls who roam Cairo's streets until brought into police custody before being turned over to an Islahaya.[2]

---

[1] *Il Binait Dol* translates to *Those Girls*.

[2] In Arabic, *Islahaya* means to "a place to fix or correct." In reality, the Egyptian Islahayas for girls are virtual prisons, places with little or no sanitation, minimal educational opportunity, and certainly no life guidance. The boys' Islahayas, discussed in one of the chapters,

A few of Those Girls – Il Binait Dol

This picture marks only a very few girls

presently living in the Islahaya in Agouza, an inner city

suburb of Cairo. They were allowed to meet with a few

of us who visited – this was late in 2012. As can be seen

the ages of the girls in this picture range from eight or

---

run on entirely different lines. Education is provided, as are clean sanitary living conditions, and a substitute "family environment," something entirely missing from the girls' Islahayas.

nine years to young teenagers, all whose futures are uncertain.

Since the 25 January 2011 Revolution, Egypt experienced and continues to feel the effects of political upheaval.

Demonstration in Cairo during the 2011 Revolution

As of June 2013, Tahrir Square in Cairo is again filled with demonstrations this time against Mohamed

Morsi and the Muslim Brotherhood. In addition to these
demonstrations, the Muslim Brotherhood of the now
deposed Morsi government holds its own
demonstrations, often inciting violence and as of August
2013, the body count is over 500 turning what was once
called the Arab Spring into an Arab Tsunami. The final
solution hangs in the balance. At this point, no one is
certain what is in store for Egyptians and Egypt.[3]

There is now an interim government and its
stated purpose is to carve a new Egypt, an Egypt built
on a foundation of democratic principles for all
Egyptians. The Muslim Brotherhood wishes to restore
its own form of government, which just prior to Morsi's
deposition, appeared to be heading towards an Islamic
state, an Islamic dictatorship, a state which began to

---

[3] Although most of the Muslim Brotherhood leaders are now in
prison (August 2013), they have threatened another massive
demonstration in which many will most likely die for 30 August
2013.

nullify rights of women and others who desired a more democratic and open society. To date all Egyptians have been affected by the continued violence. But worst of all the tragedies affects Egypt's youth, in particular its street girls, *Il Binait Dol.*

The lives of these girls shape all levels of Egyptian society, the inhumanity of what they endure is impossible to imagine. In the West, we hear of the indignities children in less-developed areas suffer, starvation resulting from civil wars, drought, or flooding, physical abuse, sex trade, rape, prostitution, all of which stir us to anger. But our anger is safe. We are thousands of miles from these conditions, on the other side of the world. We watch television ads, appeals for help, but can shut out the real tragedies taking place so far away.

The unique aspect of Egypt's shame is that for over fifty years, Egyptian authorities have kept this a dark, dirty secret. Egypt's hidden crime of neglect lay beneath global diplomacy and public relations. But the world cannot be kept in ignorance of the treatment Egyptians mete out to their children, their homeless and destitute girls. Egypt's politicians must acknowledge and be held accountable for the neglect perpetrated on these girls before the country develops into a new Egypt.

If the plight of Egypt's street children, numbering upward between 50,000 and 200,000[4] cannot be changed, then Egypt's hopes of entering a bright new future will also be blighted by the fate of its most helpless, *Il Binait Dol, Those Girls.*

---

[4] Some estimate the number as low as 50,000, but the reality is closer to 200,000 although an accurate count has never been made, the political machinery mindful of its international image virtually forbidding such statistics any form of global exposure.

I probe the conditions of the street children, the survival techniques they develop, their gang affiliations, the horrors of rape, starvation, sex trade and introduce several of the girls telling their own stories.

It is time to change and forge new lives for all Egyptians including its street girls, *Il Binait Dol.* What can be done to improve their lives and their futures? As Egypt gropes its way toward a democratic way of life, it needs to find a common ground and correct the hidden shame of her street girls. A real democracy cannot exist if its entire people are not considered.

Like so many stories of global tragedy suffered by children, this is a plea to erase the disgrace of these unfortunate girls. Positive changes must be made so these girls might be established as respected members of Egyptian society as both society and the girls struggle for rebirth and renewal.

Chapter One

IL Binait Dol – Our Voices

Approaching the Islahaya's front gate one gets the impression of its being merely another of the buildings thronging Cairo's busy neighbourhoods. The central Cairo suburb of Agouza is just that, crowded, busy, dirty, heavy traffic, many straggling shops, hot and humid during summer months, dusty and rubbish ridden at all times, a fair representation of most of the downtown Cairo areas. The entrance to the Islahaya is a rickety gate, a bit rusty, definitely in need of paint, with a guard house in disrepair.

Entryway to the Agouza Islahaya

There is a sign over the gate which reads *Moasaffet el Agouza* roughly translated as "a school or place for education in Agouza." The term Islahaya is not used. Islahaya means something else apart from education. It refers to a "fix-it" place. The Islahayas are home to hundreds of children throughout Egypt. On first entering the Agouza Islahaya, the stench of dried urine and refuse pervades the air; it gets stronger with each step toward the building's entrance.

A tour of the facilities is essential when attempting to comprehend what these street girls undergo on a daily basis. This particular Islahaya has had the benefit of Hanna Hartmann–Hosni since about 1994.[5] Straightaway you see a wall painted brightly in a sort of modern art, graffiti style. Hanna's DEO students painted this to brighten up the entrance of a building otherwise grim and grey.

---

[5] Hanna Hartmann-Hosni is an unsung hero of Egypt. Her contributions to Egypt and its most destitute is discussed in the next chapter, but briefly, she is head librarian at the Deutsch Evangelical School in Dokki and devotes her spare time and energies to these girls and others in need.

Bright artwork provided by DEO students

To the right is the remains of a garden patch also donated and put in by DEO students. Unfortunately left to nature and time, both the colourful graffiti and the garden, with the exception of a few hardy plants, show signs of neglect. Forbidden by the Islahaya Directors to tend the garden, the girls are helpless to keep their tiny patch of green alive. Even if they had right of access, gardening or garden tools have never been part of their education nor have they been encouraged to keep their environment tidy.

The courtyard, dirty, plain, exposed to the hot Egyptian sun, is barren except for a very small trellis donated by the DEO including meagre old playground equipment. On one side of the entrance, sewage water drains into the grounds.

Remains of green space at the Islahaya

This small eight-by-ten-foot patch, dug out of the

concrete slabs, holds the remnants of flowers, plants,

and shrubs. Under Egypt's unforgiving heat and Cairo's

equally unforgiving pollution, only natures heartiest can survive. In many ways, analogous to the girls within the Islahaya walls, unwatered, unloved, and uncared for, only the strongest survive.

Inside its walls, water from broken pipes or broken toilets above stairs drips down onto the floor, staining everything in its wake. The stench gets stronger.

Hygiene and sanitary conditions completely lacking

Immediately to the right sits an old man behind

a counter (below), running what to the girls is their only

access to a store. His tin cupboard contains a few old

candy bars, melted and well past their sell-by date. As the weather gets hotter, the stench gets stronger. Inside, the walls are crumbling, flaking with damp rot from leaky pipes; the cold tile floors have not seen the working side of a mop for weeks, perhaps months on end.

Entry area into Agouza's Islahaya

Once inside, you come to the main hallway which leads to all rooms: sleeping quarters, classroom, kitchen, toilet areas, wash sinks, and a couple of mouldy showers. What you immediately see are dirt encrusted walls, floors which haven't seen mops or brooms in however long, chipped plaster, peeling paint, and worst of all mould and damp everywhere. It drips from the

ceilings, creeps into the wall crevices, the cracks, some

large enough for a small fist, covered in mildew.

Mould, graffiti, and dirt mark the Islahaya entryway

The managers attempt to keep visitors from the kitchen but I was able to sneak a picture. Inside the door sits an old bathtub, broken and dirty tiles on the floor. The tub is used to soak beans for foul and tamaya.[6] The few girls working in the kitchen do not

---

[6] Foul is the bean dish – a very common Egyptian food. Tamaya are the hot, deep-fried, bean-based bread rolls. The girls only get Tamaya on special occasions; their meals mostly consist of beans

wear kitchen gloves; with their hands in the food as they work one can only imagine the germ-fest rampant at this institution. Cooking for other Islahayas for which they earn a few Egyptian pounds per month is a privilege for a very few.

(foul), in the evenings a small piece of meat, and flat Egyptian bread. Vegetables and fruits are also rare dietary foods.

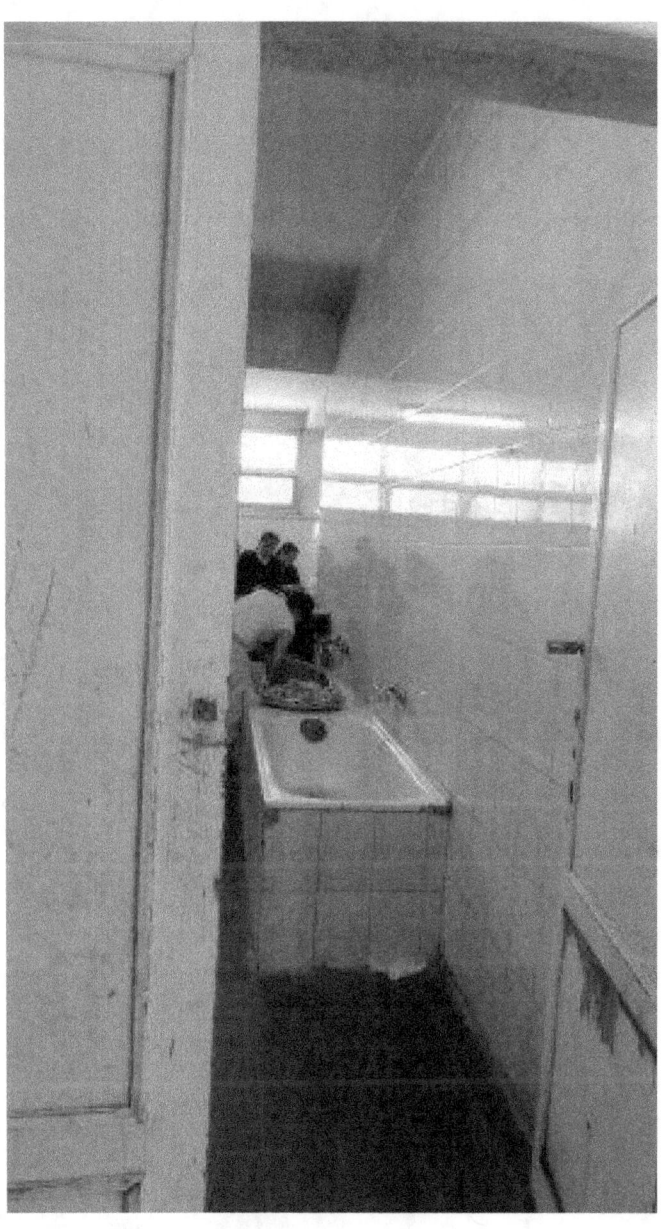

A glimpse inside the Islahaya kitchen

The kitchen is on the first floor, climbing the stairs to the second floor brings its own drama of odour, filth, and worst of all chains and gates to lock girls in against escape.

The girls are locked in – only a few can come out from behind the

bars

On my last visit in 2012, the keepers almost refused us admittance, claiming that because it was Friday, the girls rested and had no time for visitors. As we all knew this attempt to keep us out were lies, we insisted and finally they allowed us to visit with about fifteen girls.

A few of the other girls wanted to tell their stories. The stories were told over time directly to me through a very good friend and colleague, Nevien Samir. So the stories throughout the various chapters are the efforts of many visits. Nevien works in the History Department at AUC, and became interested in the girls and their plight when I asked her to accompany my students for their first visit to the Islahaya. Like most Egyptians, she did not realize the existence of these institutions. The girls trust Nevien, she is Egyptian, speaks their language, understands the language of the streets, and they know she would neither betray them to the police nor the Islahaya authorities. We sat together asking questions of those girls willing to give

us their stories.

Nevien (fourth from left) and some of the girls who told their stories

****

Sally's story as told to Nevien in 2012:

What is your name?

It's Sally.[7]

---

[7] Although Sally is not a common name in many Arab countries, many Egyptian women have this name.

Sally, how old are you? How long have you been in the Islahaya?

I think I'm twelve. My mother brought me here about four years ago. I think four years because I've had four Ramadan's here.

Sally do you remember what happened when your mother brought you here?

All I remember was that one day she pushed me out of the car when we were driving. She didn't bring me here, she left me somewhere in the middle of the city. I just stood in the middle of the street, crying, trying to run after the car, but it went too fast and I couldn't catch her.

What happened next?

I was alone, and scared all the time. I had no one; I lived on the streets for a long time, maybe even a year. I stole food, mostly bread and sometimes other food thrown out of restaurants. Sometimes I was really smart and stole money from people. I got to be very good at that. But one day a bunch of kids came and invited me to come with them. They were the first to really talk to me, so I went. They were mostly older than me, I think I might have been about nine then. They gave me real food, a place to sleep, and a job to do.

What was your job?

It was selling lemons and mint bunches on the street. I didn't mind, except that I couldn't keep the money, I had to give it to the bigger boys.

Was that all?

No, and here she really hesitated to tell us the rest, but eventually she continued. *After a while, the boys and a couple of the girls gave me something that made me feel really good, I didn't mind anything, even when the big boys came into my mattress. Everything was so really nice- warm and fuzzy.*

Do you know now what they gave you?

Yes, the madams said it was drugs, and they are haram.[8] But I liked the way they made me feel. I didn't miss my home, my family, my mother, or anyone. But I know that if they didn't give me the drugs every night then I hurt everywhere, so I had to do everything they said so they'd give them to me. I didn't care if I had food or anything else, I just needed the drugs.

Do you know how long this went on?

I'm not sure, but I just know that one day, I was selling in the streets and the police took me away. They brought me to the station and kept me there for two days. For two days I didn't have my drugs and I kept getting sick, sick on the floor, I couldn't eat or sleep.

---

[8] Forbidden

What happened next?

They couldn't make me talk, so after taking my picture, they put me in their car and brought me here to this Islahaya. I hate it here, the girls are so mean. When I first came, I wanted my drugs, I cried all the time.

Did you ever run away? Did your need of the drugs make you plan an escape?

I tried to run away, but because they thought I was crazy and being sick all the time, the supervisors locked me in a very small room and put some food in there once a day.

Did they bring in a doctor to help you get over the drugs?

No, they just called me crazy; some of the girls still call me crazy. When the supervisors aren't looking, they beat me with sticks, call me names, and try to get me in trouble.

Sally, how did you get to be in Madam Hanna's classes?

I learned not to make trouble, I just want to get out of here, learn how to read and write a little. Then maybe I can get married or something. I don't know, just anything away from here.

Will you try to find your mother?

I can't – I don't know her name or where we lived. I was only about eight when she threw me away. I've been here for four years now, where would she be? And she doesn't want me, if she did, she wouldn't have thrown me away.

Sally lives in dread of the future, she told her story in 2012, to date she manages to keep on the right side of the supervisors and is still allowed to take classes, but her future is uncertain, with no name, no identity, no papers, she can never even take the *Adadaya*. Some of the other girls still call her *mezhnuun* [crazy]; she has few friends, no confidantes. She is not *mezhnuun*, but a young girl put through more pain than any child should suffer. Sally remains isolated. Her education is a corrective tool, so that once back on the streets, she will have some resources. Her drug dependency so far is suppressed, she has not attempted to escape, but will this be permanent?

Sally today[9]

****

Behind the mouldy walls many secrets exist

which the keepers wish to bury. Their domain, their

---

[9] Sally wanted us to take her picture; for some of these girls it becomes a symbol that someone cares enough to take an interest. She told her story, a bit reluctantly in some places, but is proud of her achievements over the past few years.

rules, their wards, their prisoners. The girls quickly learn how to achieve favour with supervisors, which one can help them get privileges, with whom can they sell sex for an illicit night on the streets, who will listen to stories about others in exchange for an illegal cigarette, a phone call, an extra ration of food.

Il Binait Dol, those girls, quickly learn the system, how to behave in front of supervisors. Some of the supervisors, with nothing much to do all day enjoy punishing the girls. They slap the girls for swearing; they kick the girls if they get into a physical fight, if a girl attempts to run away, her head is shaved or she is chained to a bed.[10]

****

We were told Heya's story in 2011:

---

[10] Of all the punishments, shaving the head is the most insulting. The girls value their hair; it's the one possession they have of which they can be proud, adorn themselves, decorate if they are lucky enough to have ribbons or hair ornaments.

We will call this next girl Heya. At the time of this telling in 2012 Heya was about fourteen years old and had been in the Islahaya for almost eight years. We learned her story from one of the supervisors directly involved with Heya. The supervisor told the story but asked us please, not to tell her name, as she would lose her job and maybe not get another.[11] The story is related in Heya's voice.

I tried to escape from this place many times. The first time it worked, I ran away, but it didn't last long. I was only out for a day; then the police caught me, brought me back here to the Islahaya. When I came back, Madam Ibtisam slapped me so hard that I spit in her face.

Did you think this was the right thing to do?

I didn't care, she hurt me – called me evil names just for running away.

---

[11] This was not the girl's first attempt at running away; each time the punishment gets more stringent.

What did she do then?

She locked me in a small room, it didn't have any windows, and then she had the supervisors chain me with irons on my legs. I couldn't run, could hardly walk. There was a dirty mattress on the floor with no blankets and a bucket to use as a toilet. They put some foul in my room once a day and also one cup of water.

How long were you in this room?

I'm not sure, but it was a long time, maybe a month. When I was in there, one of the supervisors came in and shaved my head. She was really nice, didn't want to do it, but Madam Ibtisam ordered her to. This supervisor tried to clean the room a little, brought some other food and a small blanket. I know that if Madam Ibtisam found out, the supervisor might lose her job, so I didn't tell on her, even when they let me out and tried to make me talk about who brought the blanket.

Were you going to obey Madam Ibtisam and not try to escape again?

Never! I hate it here, I hate her. She's an evil woman who doesn't care at all about us. So I tried again to escape, but this time, someone must have seen me, because I didn't get past the guard. They brought me back inside, I scratched the supervisors forcing me back inside! They locked me back in the room but it wasn't for very long this time.

Why not, what happened?

In the night some guards came and put me in a truck.

The rest of the story belongs to a supervisor who told us Heya's details. They put Heya in a police van and drove her off. All we know is that she has been shipped somewhere, probably to the Sinai to an Islahaya far away from Cairo. If she tries to escape and they catch her then she will be put in a real prison. Even if she escapes, it's so far from the city that she will never make it; she will be caught and punished. We have never heard about her since.

****

When there is a general punishment, the girls cannot move beyond the locked and gated bars on the second floor where their dormitories are located. Sometimes, if the girls get rowdy, the supervisors will cane the girls, especially those they believe to be leaders, and then they declare a general lock-up, usually for a day or two, sometimes a week. During that time, none of the girls may leave the rooms, no school, no fresh air, and certainly no outside visitors, other than authorities, may enter the Islahaya.

****

Hamda told us her story in 2012:

What is your name?

It's Hamda. I'm fifteen now, but I've been here since I was eight. My mother brought me here because my father divorced her and I have too many brothers and sisters. She couldn't feed me and because I was the oldest, she brought me here. She told me that I would be better off here and she'd come and visit me all the time.

Have you seen your mother since?

She's never come here to see me, not once. I used to cry every night, waiting for her to come, but after a while, I didn't have any tears left.

When your mother brought you here, did you go to the police at all?

No, but they came and took me away for a little while. They took my picture, wrote my name down and then brought me back here.

Where did they put you, in one of the bedrooms with the other girls?

No Madam Ibtisam had me locked away in a small room; they fed me twice a day and let me out to go to the toilet three times a day. I just want to go home, I have two brothers and two sisters, and I wanted to be with them and my mother. But that never happened. One day, when

I cried too much, the supervisors came in the room and beat me with a stick, then with a chain, and then they only gave me food one time a day. So I stopped crying.

Why did they lock you in this room?

The supervisor who let me out said that I was going to live here; she said that Madam Ibtisam kept me separate until she was told I would stay here and not go somewhere else. She didn't want me to escape.

How is life here now?

I hate it here; I wish my mother would come back. But I learned to stop crying, and now the supervisors let me take classes with Madam Hala. We even took one trip to Ras Sudr with Madam Hanna. That was so nice, but life here is really bad. Except for classes, they won't let us do anything. Sometimes some of the older girls bully us, try to climb in our mattresses, and do things to us. I hate that too.

What do you want to happen if your mother doesn't come back for you?

I want to take classes and pass my exams, maybe get work outside. So I work hard and try to do my best, stay out of the way of the bad supervisors, and just do what I have to.

Hamda has little chance of taking her exams since she doesn't know her family name or where she comes from in Cairo. She has to have that information to receive identity papers-without these papers she cannot take exams, get work, or even get married.

****

Many girls, all ages, will sneak into other's beds not for comfort, but to force sexual relations on girls, usually older to younger girls. The girls receive no education in sexuality, they merely learn it is *haram*, in many ways making it more enticing for the girls in spite of the severe punishments they receive if caught. If not able to be with a partner, the girls begin masturbation. The Islamic belief that masturbation and same sex relationships are seen as abnormal and certainly *haram* is evident in that they learn early not to get caught, sneak at night or anytime when the supervisors are otherwise engaged. Most of the girls, not allowed to attend school, locked in the upper rooms, have so little to occupy them that becoming part of an inside gang, practicing illicit acts, and exerting power over girls selected as more model residents, becomes the norm. So as in most institutions a gang rises to the top, a gang of girls which terrorizes others in a bid for some sort of power.

****

The Boys

In another part of Cairo, not too far from Cairo University, is another Islahaya. This one provides a home for street boys, boys in circumstances similar to the girls. They have been abandoned, run away from home, orphaned, and left to fend for themselves; eventually captured and brought to the Islahaya by the police. There the similarity ends. Home to over 300 boys at any given time, the boys receive entirely different treatment; a helpful reception awaits them on their entry into the Islahaya. They receive instructions from supervisors, immediately given their own well-cared for bed, properly cleaned linens and coverings. From the start, the space is private and personal; no one has the right to interfere. Each bed is separated by a small shelf, place for personal items and books. As you drive into the boys' Islahaya, a large working fountain on a manicured green lawn forms the entrance. It is surrounded by green gardens, grounds well-kept, manicured, flowers, shrubs, a tiny oasis inside Cairo's smog and pollution. No rubbish can be detected in the car park, inside the entry, proper offices house the director, his staff, secretaries, and other workers who keep this Islahaya running.

The boys' Islahaya area

Entrance to the boys' Islahaya in Cairo

Once inside, the Islahaya has a section with proper classrooms for primary school children. I visited the classes, the boys, all in school uniforms, attended classes provided with desks, books, writing materials, and government trained teachers. They take the government exam, the *Adadaya,* after passing grade six. Later those interested can choose to go outside to higher education, or if not interested in academic training they will be sent to various apprenticeships. They will all receive official government ID's even if they do not know their families or family names.

Boys at play

****

Ashraf's story - told in 2006:

This is Ashraf's story. He was five in 2006. The story was told to my male students who did their practical experience at this Islahaya.

How did you get to this Islahaya Ashraf?

I don't know, I don't remember my family or anything.

Do you like it here?

Yes, I love to be here, the big boys take good care of me. The food is nice, I go to school now and am learning how to read and write.

What would you like to do after you leave here?

I want to get work and have a nice life. But not yet, I am having too much fun here.

Do you ever get punished?

Sometimes when I do things I'm not supposed to do, but mostly the big boys don't let me get in trouble. They call me their little brother!

Ashraf was brought by the police to the Islahaya as an orphan, a street child, so he does have a record and like many of the other boys, no identity other than his first name. But in the Islahaya he found acceptance from the older boys, became a kind of mascot to them.

They care for him, make sure he escapes punishment for some of his boyish pranks; generally see that no harm comes to him. For the most part, the boys protect one another; feel secure in the knowledge that even though they are in custody until the age of eighteen, they have an educational programme which provides them a way out. Literacy, training, and apprenticeships form their daily lives and eventually they will leave with an education and a clean record including an official government ID.[12]

---

[12] This ID is their passport to life, a passport which allows them to vote, travel, and most importantly work.

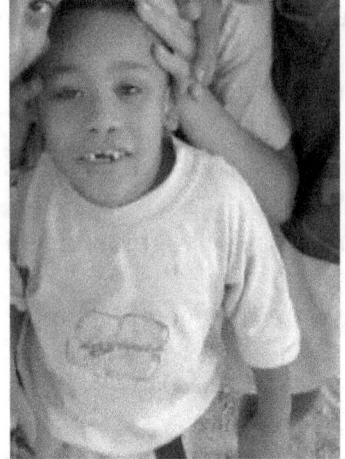

Ashraf at five

Boys enjoying play time

As part of our visits to this Islahaya, the Director

spoke with all of us whenever we needed information.

This openness differed from the secrecy we found at the Agouza Islahaya. The Directors at the girls' Islahaya have no secretarial staff; no clean office space or trained assistants. Most of all they appear to have no interest in seeing that the girls receive the best the government can provide.

Mr Ashraf, the boys' director in 2006, made sure that the boys were educated, had clean facilities, three good meals a day plus snacks, and a library in which they can sit and work. A sense of well-being, order, and purpose permeates the boys and the atmosphere of their Islahaya.

In addition to their education and other homelike care, the boys have large well-kept grounds, inclusive of playing fields, basketball court, and an area for football. The boys are not confined to their rooms, not chained to their beds, nor are they locked in small holding rooms. This is not to say they do not receive punishment, for the rules there are strictly enforced. Rough language, contraband of any kind, attempting to escape, lying, and other forms of illicit behaviour are most certainly punished. But the boys feel much more content, knowing they will eventually become valuable members of the greater community with hard work and personal effort.

****

Ahmed's story as told to my students in 2006:

My name is Ahmed; I am now fifteen years old and have been here since I was eleven.

Why did you come to the Islahaya Ahmed?

It was private problems. I ran away from home, and the police caught me. They brought me here to Mr Ashraf.

Is Mr Ashraf kind to you?

Usually he is, but if we disobey his rules, he beats us. He does this himself; none of the supervisors or teachers is allowed to hurt us.

Have you ever been beaten?

When I first came, all the time, because I really didn't want to stay, so I wouldn't do what he said, I wouldn't go to classes, and if I did, I was not good in the classrooms. But after a while, I saw how nice it was here, clean, really good food, and nice clothes to wear. Also, I didn't have the problems I had at home.

Ahmed, can you tell us about your home problems or is it too painful.

I guess I can now, since it was so long ago. My uncles and a couple of my cousins raped me from when I was very little. I hated them to touch me, I begged my father to stop them, but he just laughed and said I

shouldn't be so 'pretty'. I couldn't take it anymore, so one

day I just left home and kept walking. I stayed out for a

few nights before the police grabbed me off the streets.

Did you tell the police?

I tried to but they didn't care, they just took my

picture, and brought me here to Mr Ashraf.

So now that you're happy here, what are your

plans for the future?

When I finish my Adadaya studies, Mr Ashraf says

that I can go and become an apprentice on the outside. I

love working with computers, so I hope to get a good job

and then maybe get married.

Ahmed, would you ever marry a girl from an

Islahaya?

No way! They are really awful, and they don't get papers the way we do. They have no money, nothing, I want to marry a real girl and have my own family. I will never let my sons suffer like me.

By this writing in 2013, it can be assumed that Ahmed fulfilled his dreams. After Mr Ashraf left as Director of the Islahaya, the new Director refused to let us come in to visit with his boys. He gave no reasons, but said his children didn't need outside help, nor did they need gifts, used clothing or other things as he provided these things quite adequately out of his government budget.

****

The Girls

How can they get out? Is there a way?

Marriage is virtually the only way out for the girls, but how can they find a marriage partner, when they cannot leave the Islahaya, when they are marked with a police record, and worst than all, have no family or family identity. Who will marry the girls? Marriage is also an important aspect of life for the boys. They all want to have families, especially children which are an intrinsic part of Egyptian life, but they wish to marry girls who have families with respectable prospects. Cost for marriage is high and poor boys from the Islahaya must work hard to even come close to raising enough money to provide for their prospective brides. Since the revolutions of 2011 and now well in to 2013, it's becoming increasingly difficult for poor young people to marry, a further cause of frustration with the economic downturn in Egypt.

Would the boys from an Islahaya marry an Islahaya girl? When my students asked the boys at the

Islahaya if they would ever consider marrying an Islahaya girl, the response without exception was a resounding 'no'. To these boys marriage to a girl from the Islahaya would do nothing but keep them in the lowest strata of society. These prison girls, these Islahaya girls are not virgins. A vital facet for acceptable marriage in the Muslim world is a girl's virginity. Then too, they have no real identity, even if they have family, family shunned them. They have no money, no ability to gain possessions, and virtually no education, so why would a boy on his way up want to marry a girl with nothing?[13]

****

Hosna's story from the girls' Islahaya as told to my students in 2006.

---

[13] The safety of his environment must be qualified as there are some boys in the Islahaya, just like the girls, who refuse to submit to order and discipline, break the rules, and threaten some of the boys who comply with Islahaya rules.

I've been here for five years and I am scared all the time. The big girls threatened me; they climbed into my bed at night. They used things on me. I know I should be brave, because I'm already seventeen, but because I'm small, they treat me like a child.

How did you get here Hosna?

When I was twelve, my mother just threw me out of the house. I don't know why, she just didn't want me. I have older brothers and one younger sister, but she never liked me, so one day she just put some things in a plastic bag and said, get out 'ímshi'!

Do you like taking classes with Madam Hala?

Not really, I mean, they're nice and it gets me out of the room, away from the bully girls who really scare me. I'm tired of being scared, tired of beatings, my mother beat me all the time and so do the supervisors if I play

Tabba too much.[14] Sometimes we get to take a trip with Madam Hanna's students so going to classes is okay. But I really just like playing Tabba and I want to get married to get out of here.

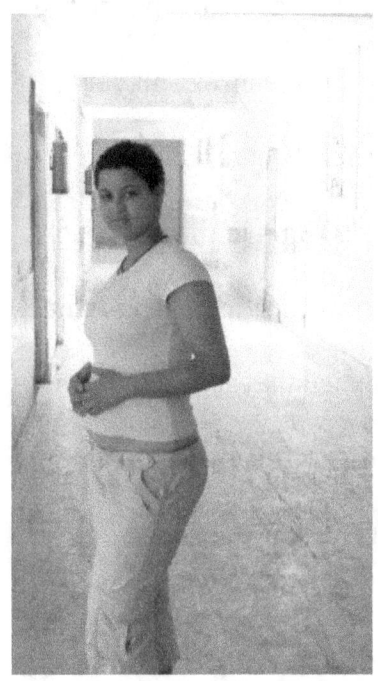

Hosna in 2011 – still no hope of leaving

****

---

[14] Tabba is a gambling stick game, very popular with Egyptian youth.

In Agouza, Madame Merwette, the current director since 2012, vetoes any outings, privileges, sometimes cancels school for the fifteen eligible girls for her own reasons. She often refuses entrance to visitors, including those from the DEO who come to engage the children in games or play in their meagre courtyard. In this she is seconded by the other directors, Madam Zeinab and Madam Naglaa who come in the afternoons. Madam Naglaa wishes to restrict the girls even further by insisting that Hanna supply galabayas rather than the regular street clothes worn by the girls and donated by DEO students and other friends of the Social Committee.

Egypt does not have a dress code for its women; they choose the style of clothing they wish to wear. If wearing the tradition galabaya is their choice, if covering their hair with the ejab is what they wish, then this is personal, not enforced. Hanna decidedly refused to fall in with Madam Naglaa's request, not on religious grounds, but because it must be the girls' choice. The Islahaya has no rules to the contrary, and she believes the girls are restricted enough. Selecting their own clothes, however slim the choices or how used the clothing, gives the girls one tiny sense of freedom and individuality.

Inside its mouldy walls and cracking ceilings, the girls waste the minutes, hours, days, months, and years wishing their lives away. With little or nothing to do, fights develop, enemies are made, friendships breakup, often beatings occur. Much of this behaviour develops because the girls sit in boredom and fear. Not always fear of someone, but of the unknown. What will happen to them, where will they be in ten, fifteen years? Will they end up like Zeinab, a resident who's been there over fifty years?

What are their hopes and dreams? Virtually all say marriage, as they know it is the only way out for them. They want a home which comes with the obligation of children that the girls see as security. From where do they hope to get their husbands? Some girls continue to sneak out at night meeting up with old street gang comrades. But in truth these boys only use them for sex, but the girls believe that it's love.

****

Mona's story as told to Nevien in 2011:

Mona's life as a street child began in 2000 when she was ten.

Mona, how did you end up here at the Islahaya?

My mother died when I was nine. We lived with my aunt and some cousins. They didn't like me at all – one day they just put me in the car and dropped me somewhere in the middle of Cairo. I didn't know where I was or where we lived. So I was alone and had to survive somehow.

And how did you survive?

That first night I had no place to sleep and I was so hungry and alone. I went into an alley and found a warm pile of rubbish. I slept there and covered up with some cardboard. The next few days were worse but after about a week some boys and girls picked me up. They said I could join them if I wanted.

So I did. They gave me food and a place to sleep and all I had to do was sell tissues during the day. As long as I turned over all the money, everything was fine, but one day I didn't have enough, at least that's what they said and one of the older boys beat me. That was my first beating but not my last.

Why didn't you run away from the gang?

I was so scared and they were better than being alone again.

What happened next?

I think it was about a year later that the boys sold me.

What do you mean "sold" you?

They gave me to an older man who took me somewhere and had sex with me. Then he brought me back to the gang and they gave me to someone else for the same thing.

Mona, how long did this go on?

I don't really know, but finally I couldn't take it anymore and ran away.

Where did you go?

I went to the police. I couldn't read, but I know who the police are.

What happened next?

Do I really have to say? It's so hard and if Madam Hala or Merwette hears this they will be very angry.

No one at the Islahaya will know this story.

Well, the police took me to the station and kept me in a back room, locked up so I couldn't run away. Every night one of the police came in and raped me. They laughed when I cried.

How did you get out of this trap?

They finally got tired of my crying I guess, so they just took my picture and brought me to this Islahaya where I've been ever since.

This isn't the end of your story is it?

No – the rest begins now really - Nevien, I am so happy.

Why are you happy now?

I am going to be married and I'm going to take the Adadaya. Madam Hanna found my family for me and the record of my birth so I can have official papers. But one day about six months ago, one of Madam Hanna's volunteer mothers saw me when she came here. She was looking for a bride for her son. She told me that I was pretty and would I like to meet her son? I was very happy to and when I met him, he was really nice. He works with repairing air conditioners and it's a good job and he wants to marry me. Madam Hanna organized some furniture for me to bring to the marriage. I am so happy.

When will you be married?

We were supposed to be married next month (June 2011) but we have to wait for his older sister to get married. I'm not sure why but that's what his mother wants, so he says we should be able to get married by September (2011).

Do you know where you will live after you get married?

We don't have enough money, or he doesn't, to buy us a place of our own so we will live with his mother until we can save enough money.

Over the summer, Mona was ecstatic, planning for her wedding, taking the *Adadya* which she passed, and planning a September wedding. Hanna found some used furniture for the newlyweds, and some other small things for her to bring to the marriage. But as of September 2011 she was not married and by December 2011 the young man told her the wedding was off. He said 'you are from the Islahaya and are not good enough for me'.

But there is more. Mona didn't want to tell the rest of her story but Nevien coaxed it out of her. By February 2012, she was introduced to another young man who offered her marriage. Again her hopes were raised, only to be dashed once again with pretty much the same excuse. She was an Islahaya girl and not worthy of him. For a second time in less than six months Mona was crushed emotionally. It began to take its toll. It shows in her appearance. Once very proud of her clothes, though used, always neat, she tried to be stylish. Her hair was well-groomed; she took pride in her learning. By early summer 2012 her whole demeanor changed. Mona's future and really her life are in jeopardy.

Mona in 2011

As of 2013, Mona is still in the Islahaya but

finding it more and more difficult to hope. Mona's

chances of getting out have changed. Pretty, bright,

loving her education, Mona thought marriage would be

her destiny. It almost was, twice, but twice now she has been rejected. She's an Islahaya girl with nothing to offer. Mona has become harder since the last rejection over a year ago; even though she's passed her *Adadaya* she knows that further education is out of the question. There is no money for high school, where can she live; can she stay in the Islahaya? Will this to be her permanent home?

****

A few girls have left the Islahaya through marriage; sometimes a family member on the outside feels sympathy and arranges a marriage. Jumping at any opportunity to leave, a girl accepts. What happens to her afterwards is difficult to tell, the girls do not return to the Islahaya even for a visit, and if they do, it's because they are lonely. The husband's family is not welcoming; she has no friends on the outside, no one with whom to talk. So, one or two of the girls will take the long bus ride to the Islahaya for human contact, a place where they once had friends and any sort of family. It is the rare man who is willing to risk his future with a wife from the lowest part of society and even if he does wish to marry her, the girl must pass his family's approval, in particular that of his mother, as she will be the one most closely associated with his new wife.

What alternatives are available for *Il Binait Dol?* When they reach twenty-one, they can leave the Islahaya but where will they go, what can they do? If they have received the minimal education, passing their *Adadaya* exams, this still leaves them floundering. Training for work beyond making a few pots and weaving a few simple bags is virtually non-existent in the Islahaya. They have no notion of housework, so they cannot hire themselves out as cleaners, most of the girls cannot cook, only a few gained the right to work in

the kitchen and then the majority of the food was foul

and sometimes tamaya. If they cook for wealthy people,

their skills must surpass simple Egyptian fare they've

eaten and prepared in the Islahaya. For this, they have

no training. Most families refuse to employ girls from

their backgrounds, with police records stuck to them

throughout their lives. In spite of the education which a

few girls receive from the attentive instruction and care

from Hanna's teachers Madams Hala, Wafaa, and Ingy,

employment will be difficult, police records

notwithstanding.

Il Binait Dol often lash out in frustration,

especially the older girls, they know their time at the

Islahaya is ending, where in spite of the conditions, they

have a place to sleep which is not on the streets and

have three meals a day. Walls crack around them,

ceilings leak dirty water, pipes break, the toilet is filthy, and showers are rare, but they do not have to wander the streets, they do not have to put their hands out for a crust of bread or a piaster, they do not have to steal. But as they near twenty-one they do have to worry about tomorrow, because for them it does come and often comes too soon. In spite of attempts to run away, when they can take their freedom and walk out the front gate, past the guards many of whom have used them for sex, what is their direction, where can they go? One sure option is back on the streets. But if and when caught, they will not see the inside of an ill-kept Islahaya again; they will see the devastating walls and gates of an Egyptian prison for women.

Chapter Two

Hanna – Egypt's Unsung Hero

I first met Hanna Hartmann-Hosni in 2005. We sat next to each other as members of the Cairo Choral Society and from that time on became fast friends. I soon learned about Hanna's work with the various causes affecting Egyptians. She knew I was going to teach a Gender course at the American University and with Hanna's usual aplomb, she immediately thought that I should visit the Islahaya in Agouza. It would be a great place to bring my students. They could help for a few hours during the semester. Did I want to go to this place, which she had described in detail? I gulped, said okay, let's do it, and went along on her next visit. I so admired Hanna, she seemed fearless. What if the Madam's wouldn't let us in, and when we got inside, what would I do? I'd only been in Cairo a few short months and had no Arabic beyond good day and directing taxi drivers. How would I communicate with the girls?

What met my senses nearly made me turn and run. Hanna thought that perhaps I could bring my students to visit the Islahaya? How could I expect girls from very privileged backgrounds to help girls in a place that smelled worse than a sewer? What would their families say; let alone the University's reaction to this venture? But Hanna virtually pushed me up the staircase to the locked gates and then to the classroom where about ten girls were receiving some lessons. I don't know to this day whether they were as overwhelmed as I to a stranger, a Westerner, visiting their classroom, but their reaction is one that I can never forget. I had my camera, and they clambered for pictures to be taken. This is what met my eyes.

From that moment on, the barriers dropped: language and fear. All I thought about concerned their tiny existence, with no one to care if they lived or died, but here came someone new, someone who wanted to capture their essence on film, talk with them even though we couldn't communicate in the same language. This is what Hanna has been about for so many years, effectively struggling on her own to bring a bit of light to these young girls of Cairo's streets. Alone she champions these girls, fights with government ministers to change the worst of their living conditions. These girls, *Il Binait Dol,* deserve humane treatment the same as anyone else. Hanna knew this from the beginning.

Hanna Hartmann-Hosni (far right)

and two Islahaya madams

Hanna Hartmann-Hosni first visited the Agouza Islahaya with a colleague in 1994. *'When I saw the conditions there immediately I felt I must do something about this. The street children lived in filth alongside mentally retarded children, none of whom had any help or anyone to care what happened to them. All were thrown in together, their rooms were dirty, many shared a single, very unclean mattress, and non-existent sanitary conditions forced the children to live in cesspits for disease.'*

'I began small projects to raise money to buy mattresses (shown below) and beds then began to work on how to fix the unsanitary conditions.'

Mattresses for the girls – money donated to Hanna by a former DEO student

Hanna Hartmann-Hosni and girls of the Islahaya

In all her efforts Hanna encounters resistance
from the madams and government officials. The school
provided virtually nothing; the governmental teachers
did and do nothing except sit around drinking tea with
the supervisors. A plethora of problems faced Hanna
and continue to mount with each change or
improvement she attempts to make.

Working tirelessly as the Head Librarian at her
school, the Deutsch Evangelical Ober Schule (DEO) in
the Cairo suburb of Dokki, Hanna has energy and to
spare for those less fortunate than herself. Hanna spurs
everyone in her path, friends, students, colleagues, to
participate in the many drives and functions she
establishes to help the street children. In addition she
sponsors efforts to help outcast members of leper
communities. Currently she's embarked on a crusade to
aid the hundreds of Syrian refugees crowding into
Cairo. Anyone who knows Hanna understands her zeal

and integrity. None of what she accomplishes and works for is for personal acclaim or gain; it comes from her heart, and all goes to the underprivileged.

Rallying forces to help in her charitable work demands energy, commitment, time, and most of all heart. Married to an Egyptian, with two sons of her own to raise, Hanna saw a people in so much need that in compassion and passion she reached out to those who suffer every day. It is due to her humanitarian efforts through the years that old and young alike have Hanna to thank for the small comforts which they now receive.

Hanna, unlike many who engage in humanitarian efforts, is not a woman of independent wealth or power, nor a woman of leisure. Interspersed around her very busy life as Head Librarian, raising her two sons, being a wife, friend, and participant in community activities, Hanna's wish to make life better for as many as possible occupies any open compartment in her daily routine.

For her it began when a colleague brought her to Abou

Zhabel, an area in Babaluk near Cairo, for lepers. What

she saw changed how she planned her life in Egypt as

attested to by the results of her first trip to Abou Zhabel.

Locked in – Abou Zhabel

Living conditions at Abou Zhabel

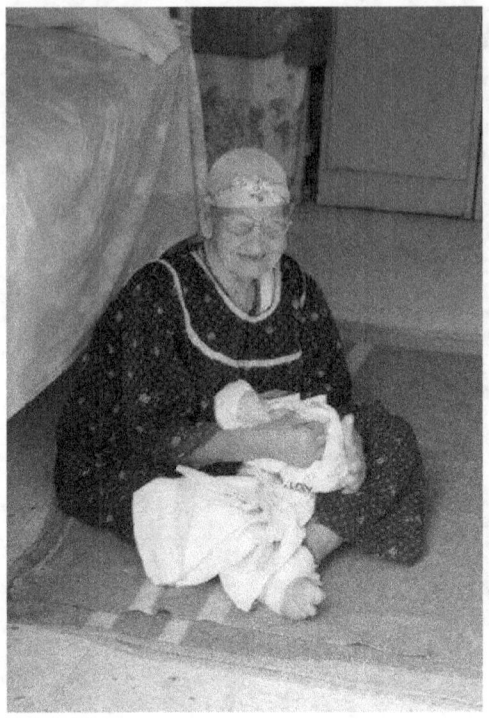

A resident at Abou Zhabel

When first asked by a colleague to accompany a small group of volunteers, Hanna knew no hesitation. What she found there stirred her compassion and from that time on she continues her vigorous campaigns against deprivation, poverty, and corruption in high places. For her the most painful of all her activities other than witnessing the horrors in which Egypt's destitute live, is the difficulty of scrambling for donations of time and money. Egypt is Hanna's adopted home, although she continues close ties with family and friends in her native Germany and ironically it is many of her friends in Germany who contribute financially on a regular basis rather than the Egyptian government or wealthy Egyptians.

Children at Abou Zhabel – caught in the trap

Although Hanna possesses a warm heart, an abundance of vitality, a coterie of volunteers, it needed much more than this to amalgamate all her causes into a cohesive unit. That's when she realized the necessity of forming a committee to manage the donations she receives; act as the principle foundation for the fund raising projects initiated and carried out again by students and volunteers, and give her activities the legitimacy needed for local and international recognition. The Committee oversees the activities, implements new initiatives for fund raising, in addition to giving students at the DEO a recognized activities club. Note the problem facing NGO's. They are under the hammer at the moment; the Egyptian government stops or prevents much of their work from being accomplished. Some have been closed down, and others' works have been drastically limited. Hanna does better because she is not an official NGO nor does she have any overhead. All the money she receives goes directly to her causes. There are no administrative costs as she takes nothing for herself. However, she does document every cent spent on the Islahayas and the other causes for which she raises money. The government has an accounting from her as per their requirements.

A major obstacle to her charities is the Egyptian government itself. Officials object to her efforts, she often has to take on ministers at the highest level to overcome the many blocks put in her way. But Hanna refuses to take defeat at the hands of those in power; she pursues her goals with vigilance.

Another leper community in Belbeis, a small village near Ismalaya in the eastern desert close to the Sinai Peninsula is visited by Hanna and members of the Social Committee at least twice a year. Students and adult volunteers spend hours making small care packages containing bars of soap, shampoo, other toiletries, clean towels, pillows, and items necessary for small comforts. In her twice annual visits she supplies fresh fruits and vegetables or juices, a real dietary necessity which residents of the communities don't often receive. Run by the Sisters of St Vincent de Paul and partially funded by Caritas, this leper community's population exceeds 300.

Hanna (far left) with one of the nuns and a volunteer at Belbeis

Hanna's Social Committee volunteers

delivering supplies to Abou Zhabel

Examples of the conditions Hanna works to alleviate

at the leper communities

A resident at the leper community

Thankful for the small gifts of supplies

Hanna's group brings to Abou Zhabel

These residents are no longer contagious, but once declared a leper, even though medication has contained the disease, these people have nowhere to go. Their old villages and communities won't take them back, they must stay. Stunted, deformed, many with loss of limb, they are unable to work on the outside. They also live with the knowledge of how their general appearances affect those on the outside. Life holds nothing for these sufferers. In attempts to achieve some form of normality, many lepers have married and have children. They do arts and crafts, weave simple carpets, make souvenirs to be sold in the markets; thereby earning a few Egyptian pounds, but not enough to sustain a real life. Unfortunately their children too are condemned to life within the community as families from their former villages refuse to allow "leper" children in their lives. They won't tell us their stories, but pictures reflect the old adage about a "thousand words."

On our visits, I personally witnessed the smiles which lit up residents' faces when they meet the DEO school children. It's obvious to any who see that these people live in utter loneliness, beyond reach of the outside world. Hanna and her students bring some small joys to lift their sadness.

Charities, in this case Caritas, started a kindergarten for the children of those living in Abu Zhabel. Within their two kilometre square area the residents of Abu Zhabel are virtually imprisoned. The Social Committee gives support with supplies, school materials and moral comfort. It contains 650 hospital inmates, 180 children in kindergarten. The village population consists of Muslims and Christians as both communities refuse to care for lepers. While Hanna's students visit for a few short hours feel they are not neglected or forgotten. You can see they particularly love the children, its life, young life, taking time to remember these forbidden few. The effects of the disease can be terrifying to school children, but Hanna and their parents refuse to let these students go through life hiding from this reality.

Hanna's Social Committee supplies what materials they can gather for the children attending the schools at Abu Zhabel. Sometimes their kindness comes from the DEO which allows Hanna to bring old books and other discarded materials to supplement meagre supplies and materials. At present, conditions for these residents of the Abou Zhabel village have no hope for change; their situation remains the same as it was prior to the revolution and it appears that no change is imminent.

Hanna's multi-layered fundraising ventures range from selling handcrafted goods made by the residents of Abou Zhabel, objects crafted by the girls from Agouza's Islahaya, a Charity Pyramid Run for which Hanna had to approach the Ministry of Police and the Ministry of Tourism for permission of upwards of 5000 runners to participate. Her students have a stall every year at the DEO Christmas Bazaar and sell cloth carry bags, arts and crafts, and other handiwork. Just recently, when Hanna became aware of the injured from the revolution, many who needed surgery and immediate medical care but could not pay, she instantly conceived an idea. A German jewellery designer, Babl Shoekermann designed a lovely pin, donating the design to Hanna's Committee for their fundraising needs. Babl Shoekermann, a former Cairo resident and colleague of Hanna's, donated several other designs to Hanna's various projects.

Hanna searched out a silversmith in the Khan el Khalili willing to create a simple "revolution" pin from silver with a small coral rose. She convinced him to donate his time. The pin is lovely, simple, and indicates support for the revolution. The profits from this venture alone skyrocketed into thousands of Egyptian pounds, every bit going for the medical costs of revolution victims.

But her funds stretch even further. A very

difficult task, yet Hanna's frugality to stretch each

pound to its limits enables her to provide teachers for

the Islahaya.

Silver and coral "Revolution" pin

A little more than ten years ago Hanna's

Committee found, paid for, and continues to provide

two excellent teachers for the girls.[15] These teachers,

qualified and hard-working, chose not to work for the

government, but engaged in private tutorials when

Hanna first met them. They agreed to work for Hanna's

Social Committee and begin the arduous task of

teaching these illiterate street girls. Hanna must

provide not only a salary, but money for their pensions,

holidays, and medicare, as per the Egyptian laws. This

she does, the money is donated by former German

colleagues who find it within their hearts and financial

ability to send checks amounting to 215 Euros (about

278US) each month, to provide for these teachers.

Unfortunately, the Revolution had and is having

negative effects on Hanna's ability to raise funds for the

girls. Now with the problems at the Pyramids with

---

[15] They now have three full-time teachers and one part-time teacher for the few girls able to take the Adadaya exam (the exam between junior and senior high school equivalent). The part-time teacher is specifically for language as this is now a requirement to take the exam.

vendors and increased violence, Hanna's charity run is also in danger of failing. Hanna needed luck – which came. First, a friend who wanted to take part from a distance, sent Hanna 200 Euros (258US), then a church group from Germany read the DEO website, felt the cause was truly worthy, and sent 330 Euros (426US). Next a lady and her group members who were fasting prior to Easter sent 500 Euros (645US). All these donations came from Germany. Her Social Committee established a website, again courtesy of the DEO www.Deokairo.de, which lists their activities and fundraising needs. As it is from the DEO, a German school, all projects are listed in German with English translations.

Hanna's ingenuity and resourcefulness find avenues for funding her projects beyond the norm. For example, late in 2008 Hanna learned of a competition instituted by the German based pharmaceutical company Sanofi Pasteur. This company announced the possibility for one organization or school to receive a prize of 10,000 Euros (12,917US). The prize would go to an organization or group whose activities demonstrated caring and philanthropic work with children. As it is a German company any German school group or organization could participate in the competition.

Hanna organized her DEO students to make a video of their work, secretly photographed inside the Islahaya, wrote reports, they filed everything in the hope that they might receive even one of the lesser prizes. In 2009 an ecstatic Hanna phoned me to say she and her Social Committee had won the major prize and she would be flown to Germany to receive this honour. Every cent of the 10,000 Euros has been used for her Islahaya children and other schools. They bought mattresses for over 100 girls, paid for small excursions with a sum set aside for a projected Red Sea outing in 2010. Hanna purchased food, drinks, fruits, and vegetables for the girls. Out of 181 schools and organizations participating in the competition, Hanna took top prize, a real victory. But one victory does not last forever; Hanna must always seek the next pound. The competition's name *Kinderwelten Teilen lohnt,* under the auspices of a general title *Children's World Sharing its Worth* saved the Social Committee and in particular lasted to provide the needed funds during the very sparse fund raising year, 2011, the year of the first Egyptian revolution.

In 2010 the Social Committee received another award, this time only a certificate from the German Bundespräsident for efforts in the competition *Alle Für eine Welt,* translated *All for One World.* The competition was a bit stiffer for this contest; Hanna's group went up against 620 Schools. Although they received no funds, a certificate from the Ministry of Development could be added to her many accolades. In addition to this, with Hanna I attended fund raising dinners at the French Embassy in Cairo where she receives recognition for her work with Egyptian children and to which she is invited every year.

Charity from the Social Committee does not end with girls' Islahayas but for years Hanna engaged her Committee and students to assist with a government school in the El Minya governorate, a school that without Hanna's assistance would have fallen into disaster years ago. I accompanied Hanna, her students and parent volunteers on an overnight trip to El Minya. Everyone at this school, parents, teachers, and students alike overflowed with joy at Hanna's visit. Egyptians are very emotional and have no hesitation in showing their feelings. Teachers and students arranged a small party with cakes and drinks for everyone before we went off to the various classrooms with supplies. On this overnight excursion, we devoted part of the trip to take some al Minya students and teachers on a short boat trip down the Nile with a picnic on board. We supplied all the food, the boat fare and tips paid for by funds raised, and spent the afternoon getting to know students and teachers from this very impoverished village school.

Children and teachers at El Minya school thank Hanna and the Social Committee.

View from the Nile boat in el Minya

During the year, the Committee collects old

books, Hanna buys notepads by the virtual truckload,

pens, pencils and small packs in which to carry these

supplies. We handed these simple gifts to students from

grades one through six. At times Hanna is able to bring

used or discarded but still workable computers and

other electronic equipment to the school, again courtesy

of the DEO. Many of the ordinary governorate schools in Upper Egypt do not receive equivalent support given to schools in Cairo or Alexandria, so without a partner school, many would not be able to offer a modicum of education to the children of Upper Egypt or the less prosperous governorates.

****

Back in Cairo, Hanna faces daily difficulties imposed by new government requirements. Recently the government demands that rather than the two teachers paid for by her Social Committee, the government now requires four for all the subjects. The girls currently get up to ninth grade education – preparing for the *Adadaya*. Their curriculum consists of math, religion, Arabic, chemistry, and English. Now they must have lessons in French but the government refuses to pay for this tuition. So that the girls may qualify for the *Adadaya* a woman named Madame

Samia, the mother of a former DEO student pays, from

her own pocket, for the services of a French teacher.

She also sees to the scheduling and supervision of the

Committee teachers.

Another difficulty for educating the girls, or at

least allowing them to sit for their exams, is identity.

Many of the girls neither know their real identity, their

home village or any relatives. A search must be

initiated and the cost of the search is something which

the government doesn't feel obliged to underwrite.

After all, these are only girls, they do not require an

education; they may get married, if anyone will have

them, and then do what females are good for, produce

children, clean house, cook meals, and perhaps work

outside the home as maids. An education for girls is

irrelevant and costly, and certainly unnecessary as is

their having any official identity cards. The investigation

costs money and what would these girls do with identity cards anyway? This seems to be the reasoning behind government refusal to invest in their *Il Binait Dol.*

****

Samira's problem

I desperately want an education, I want to sit my exams; and if the opportunity ever comes, go further in my studies. I don't want to believe that I will be stuck here in the Islahaya forever, I want to be a veterinarian, I want a real life outside. If I have to leave without an education, what is there for me? I will have to live again on the streets, become part of a gang again, boys will use me, and maybe then I will get with a baby. My life will be over. I am nineteen years old, I think, so old for this exam, but please, Madam Hanna, can you find a way out for me?'

Islahaya classroom

We know that Samira's dreams of an education, future as a doctor is only a pipe dream. There are no funds at all to send her to high school, let alone university, no one to care for her while there, she cannot stay in the Islahaya and continue an education. But at this point, rather than discourage her dreams, Hanna found the funds to initiate a search into Samira's family, her background, the village from which she came. The next step was to find whether or not her birth was announced. If announced, and in Samira's case it was, then the mayor's office recorded the information according to law. Through this Samira did obtain a birth certificate allowing her to sit for her *Adadaya*.

****

Not all the girls have Samira's ambition, nor are they all allowed to be educated above basket weaving and pottery. The Madam who runs the Islahaya determines via her own judgment who should be allowed proper schooling, to date the average is fifteen to twenty girls out of the one-hundred or so Agouza inmates.

Apart from funds for education, Hanna works diligently to give the Islahaya girls one outing on the Red Sea every year. A place not too far from Cairo, around three hours by bus, is Ras Sudr. It is not in any way elaborate, more like a camp with small huts, three or four beds to each hut. I went with Hanna and the girls one year for a one-day portion of the girls' week long holiday. Dressed in used clothes, most had no proper swim suits, eating and drinking sandwiches and juices provided by the Social Committee, the girls didn't mind at all. For one week they could breathe free air, run in the lovely waters of the Red Sea, play in the sand, and be carefree children. To provide this Hanna's Committee needed to raise about £80,000 Egyptian (11,500US). They must send not only the one hundred plus children, but the Islahaya directors and other staff as well. A small price to pay for the children's only holiday from Cairo's summer heat and pollution. A holiday to which they count the weeks, days, hours for a scent of freedom and fresh air, the Red Sea tickling their toes.

The excursion usually takes place the third week in June, perfect weather, and no hindrances to block a week of unbridled joy for the children. Yet, in the year 2011 things did not go as planned. The money was raised, it usually takes a year to get that amount of money, the camp was booked as usual, food preparations began, the girls anticipating, and then the director, Madam Samia stepped in with a forceful veto. No she said, it's too dangerous, something might happen, we cannot let the girls go.

In all of Hanna's years taking the girls to Ras Sudr, on school buses donated by the DEO, nothing has ever occurred to mar the experience. The girls have never run away, they were always safe, they encountered no problems on the road. Why then the veto? Madame Samia refused to go into details, but it appears to be too much work for her, although it is Hanna and the Social Committee who do everything

from raising the money, and booking the reservations at
the camp (exclusively for the girls). They also provide
food for the week, see that the girls have adequate
clothes for the beach, send along towels, drinks,
anything needed for the trip, and accompany them on
the first day to ensure all is well at the camp.

For over a month Hanna tried to get help and answers.
She and her husband Souhail Hosni, her greatest
supporter, wrote and phoned the director, made
appointments with the Ministry of Social Affairs
(responsible for the Islahaya), visited several times,
made impassioned pleas with all the proper channels, to
no avail. The trip for these girls was off, no more
questions, no more arguments. Below is a letter written
by Hanna in her last attempt to obtain answers. She
asked me to correct the English, but I think her own
words speak more powerfully than a correctly worded

statement. With Hanna's kind permission, I have reprinted her plea in this chapter.

'What can we do? Who can help us? Why is help for the needy being blocked by the ministry? We, the Social Committee of the German Evangelical School (DEO), have been working with the girls from Moasset el Agouza, an approved school – Islahaya - for street children, for the past fifteen years.

For years, we have been paying for four teachers, who support about twenty-five girls to pass the governmental annual exams successfully. Students, teachers and mothers from our school visit the girls in Agouza on a weekly basis thus creating an atmosphere of friendship. If they need anything - be it new mattresses, new windows, clothes, soap, toothpaste, or renovation works, we always find a way to support this approved school. We even managed to build a sports- and playground there. The girls especially enjoy excursions to a club, little boat trips on the Nile, day trips to El Fayyoum. For the last few summers we have been able to organize a five day trip to Ras Sudr for eighty girls and twenty employees. The girls start dreaming about this holiday in January. Sun, sand, sea, freedom, peace - this is what the girls often lack in their daily life in their home in Agouza.

This year, again, the DEO community raised enough money to make this trip to the Red Sea possible. We gave the invitation to the management of the Islahaya in Agouza at end of March - and three weeks ago it was suddenly rejected.

Just imagine the girls being locked in Cairo all summer, without hope. We have written letters to the different departments of the Ministry of Social Affairs, to the governor of Giza, the Gamaeya, so that the trip could still take place. The trip was again rejected, even after the management of the camp in Ras Sudr, the girls' destination, assured us that the girls would be safe. Seventy pupils from our DEO went to Ras Sudr last month - everything was perfectly safe.

This really puzzles us. Suddenly, authorities are afraid for the children's safety? Children who used to live in the streets, who are locked and castigated and mostly left to their own in what is considered an approved government school? Is this the new attitude towards these children? Better to lock them away, rather than let them experience a little joy in their miserable lives. We are very sad that this summer is so hopeless for these girls, who are our friends. We want to continue to help; we want to improve the situation of these children at least a little bit. Why are there forces that prevent us from doing so? Who are they? What is the true reason: Aren't we all one people? Shouldn't we cooperate? We are still ready. Please support us, do not put obstacles in our way. Under the old regime we were silent. We knew it would not help to speak up. However, is it not a new era we are living in now? There has been a revolution - or did everything stay as it was - or even become worse?'

Yours with regret and sincerity,

Social Committee of DEO (German Evangelical School),

Dokki

Enjoying an outing away from the Islahaya

At this point, Hanna does not know whether or not she can continue to support this Islahaya. The plumbing and bathrooms remain in unsanitary and in virtually unusable condition, the little play area they created has fallen into disrepair, the building inside and out leaks with mould and mildew, causing spores to get into the air, poisonous to the health of the girls. Without the weekly encouragement from the DEO of shampoo to wash out lice, provide toothpaste and toothbrushes, the girls, or at least the few allowed to

receive these gifts, will regress into their previously
unhealthy conditions.

On my last visit to the Islahaya, in 2012, the
police brought in a very young girl, about eight years
old, she thought. Wandering the streets with two black
plastic bags which contained the entirety of her
possessions, the police picked her up, and brought her
to Madam Samia at the Islahaya. Frightened, confused,
and most certainly illiterate, she only knew her first
name, Leyla. Hanna asked Madam Samia for permission
to bring her into the courtyard, give her some juice and
cakes, and help her get acquainted with the other girls.
Flatly refusing, Madam Samia gave the excuse that she
might be shipped to another Islahaya and therefore
could not have contact with the other girls. They
promptly marched her off and locked her in one of the
"holding rooms" where she stays while awaiting her
fate.

With the undisclosed riches in Egypt, it remains

a mystery why none of the influential and wealthy

people refuse to come down hard on the authorities

who allow children to live in these conditions. Prior to

the 2011 revolution, Hanna wrote to the first lady,

Suzanne Mubarak, for help. Mrs Mubarak claimed to be

in the forefront of women's rights, always interested in

fighting for those less privileged. Over the years, Hanna

realized, as did so many others, that this fight for justice

was mere talk.

Hanna eventually accepted defeat for the Ras

Sudr expedition and gave most of the money to Sister

Mary, a non-Coptic Christian nun who runs, single-

handedly, an orphanage within Cairo. Sister Mary's

orphanage needed a new roof and this money went a

long way to helping her get one installed. She finds

these children, who must, according to law, be under a

year old, cares for them, sees to their education, food,

training, and healthy living conditions. Sister Mary is grateful for the few donations which Hanna from time to time offers, but since she is from an influential Christian family, she receives help not only from her family but also from the Church. As her girls grow, she teaches them hygiene, gives them all chores within the orphanage, teaches them cooking, and most importantly, ensures the girls receive a real education. She has teachers who come to the school for the primary children, and then the older girls go to local governorate schools. These girls are raised as Christians because their origins are unknown, but they do have papers from the orphanage enabling them to continue education and receive health care. Sister Mary has no help; there are only the day teachers to come for lessons. When and if she finds a girl's family, they are allowed to visit during holidays if they wish, but not all families are found or known. The comparison to the treatment the Islahaya girls receive is immeasurable.

Can a country survive after the revolutions of 2011 and 2013 with only a handful of civic minded people like Sister Mary, the nuns of St Vincent de Paul at Abou Zhabel, Caritas, and the Social Committee formed and run by Hanna Hartmann-Hosni? Post revolution Egypt must address its deficiencies not just at the top level of society, not merely with elections, writing a new constitution, all of which are essential, but it needs to examine the heart of its life-blood, the millions of Egyptians without, and more significantly the thousands of children living on the street, most of whom do not have the benefit of Hanna Hartmann-Hosni to fight for them.

Hanna Hartmann-Hosni is someone who can in all sincerity be called an Egyptian hero. It is her work

which has brought many children and other poor back
from the brink of annihilation. Without her, the
Islahaya girls might have been victims of plague as they
suffer the indignities of dirt, rotten mattresses, filth, and
neglect. Yet, in spite of her years of work, the Islahayas,
though improved, still remain disease-infested
institutions.

Hanna cannot continue forever, she will retire
and when she does, who will continue her work. I have
sometimes found her in tears – tears of frustration
because she is finding it increasingly difficult to find
willing volunteers among her students and even some
members of her Social Committee. They believe in what
she is doing but giving time and energy to these
charitable pursuits is another matter. Hanna fears that
when she retires, all the years she's devoted to the girls
will be forgotten. This must not be allowed to happen.
Hanna's efforts must be maintained as the street girls

will not fade away but *Il Binait Dol* will continue as part of Egyptian society until great changes and strides are made within the seat of authority and power, the government. It needs to take responsibility, and give all the assistance at their command to Egypt's unsung hero, Hanna Hartmann-Hosni.

Chapter Three

Homeless and Helpless in Egypt

"Please sir, I want some more" - the words of despair dragged out of the orphan hero in Charles Dickens' *Oliver Twist,* a novel written about some of the social injustices in nineteenth century England, mirrors the pain felt by girls in twenty-first century Cairo. Even as the horror of social injustice found its way into the consciousness of many British during the days of its industrial Revolution, the situation then is easily more understandable than that of the terrifying hunger, poverty, abuse, and homelessness that exists in so many parts of the world today. Egypt is no exception.

Poverty and wealth within the same neighbourhoods

A country of 80 million, the largest population of Middle Eastern countries, rich in historical monuments, tombs, and pyramids, it would be hoped the government leads the way into the new century for its millions. Until the recent events of the Arab Spring, the Egyptian government received around eight billion US dollars a year in aid. Sadly for Egyptians, these US funds, meant for use in developmental programs, never rescued impoverished Egyptians or necessary programmes to strengthen the country. They mysteriously disappeared into the pockets of the regime and its closest supporters. Mubarak abused this gift from America by not putting it to use for education, health, and the general well-being of the people. Just applying one estimated figure which puts the illiteracy rate for Egyptians anywhere between 50-75% (the highest number being for women) demonstrates the pathological disregard the Mubarak regime had for its people. The monumental gap between the very wealthy privileged few and the indigent majority are as true today after the Arab Spring Revolution of 25 January 2011 and its ongoing sequel, the Revolution of 30 June 2013 as during Mubarak's rule.[16]

---

[16]As of August 2013, the Muslim Brotherhood continues in its violent demonstrations against the new interim government – the final outcome is yet to be seen.

The real Egyptian – street vendor

Among the 80 million Egyptians so much is easily hidden especially in cities boasting twisting alleyways, dark places, and spaces.

One of Egypt's most tragic secrets is the children roaming city streets, lost in the labyrinthine mazes twisting throughout Cairo and Alexandria. These children come from all over the country with one common theme in their young lives, abuse. It can be sexual abuse by fathers, brothers, any other male relative, physical beatings by parents, often step-mothers who do not want another woman's children but are bound to have them under her care. Some of these children are abandoned by indigent mothers whose husbands left or divorced them. Left in indigent circumstances they cannot support themselves or their children. With poverty at an all-time high, and crime escalating, these children, very often girls, are caught up in street gangs to sell packets of tissues, bunches of mint leaves, small bags of lemons, or forced into prostitution. Their tragically lonely lives without family, friends, or hope, are one legacy of Egypt's political regimes which these children must face each waking moment.

Unlike Oliver Twist who begged the governor for more food, Egypt's street children cannot ask for more, or even for the first morsels; there is no one they can ask. There is nothing, no food, shelter, clothing, or identity to which they are entitled. The continuum of hunger, despair, poverty, and helplessness before the Arab Spring, during the Arab Spring, and now into its failing, darkening Arab Tsunami, clearly indicates the desperation of Egypt's impoverished. Even during the initial period of hope after 25 January 2011, Egypt's street children were not even considered by Revolutionaries or by those who eventually achieved power. The Arab Spring, in all its glory and promise for freedom and democracy, never touched the lives of these children. There was and is no mention of granting the countless children roaming throughout Egypt any rights, as people, or as citizens. They are the invisible shame, the shame Egypt must keep hidden.

Hidden from public view, locked in an Islahaya with no way out

These girls live at the state's mercy, a state acting *in loco parentis*. But the Egyptian state wears blinders; it does not wish to know or certainly publicise, the tragedy of its homeless, nameless, stateless children. It is a blind parent, an unforgiving parent, with many of its officials lacking the humanity to bother about the legions of children roaming its city streets. For many, this leads to police records, and incarceration in the "fix-it" places called Islahayas. To borrow again from

Dickens, there was always an underlying element of hope for the young Oliver, a basic societal goodness, a humanitarian aspect, while Egypt's lost souls, its street children, have no expectations. Oblivious to their country's past splendour, the thousands of street children merely seek to survive. The number of street children makes a small army;[17] battles have been won with fewer numbers, the chance of survival higher in battle than that of these homeless Egyptian children, refugees in their own country.

This particularly applies to the girls, a situation compounded by the Muslim Brotherhood (while they were in brief authority) that demonstrates contempt toward women. How can a political party which limits

---

[17] Estimates reach as high as 200,000 in Cairo alone. No actual count is made, so figures can range between 50,000 and 200,000.

the lives of females ever show sympathy for girls they regard as common discards?[18]

What then is the solution for these children? What hope of relief and help can they expect? A street girl's journey begins with abandonment, sometimes gang life, and always the police, photographed and branded for life as a criminal. The officers drop girls at Islahayas leaving them to the ministrations of madams untrained in child care or any other sort of care, madams given governmental positions in a place they neither desire nor understand. Those put in charge of Islahayas for girls only bide their time waiting for government pensions. Girls are a burden to society and must be dealt with accordingly. In self-protection, the young street girls fantasize about their families, their origins, hopes, and dreams.

---

[18] This is based on a number of their unilateral restrictions placed on women during their short time in power.

One of the fantasies created by many of the girls is that of "nice ladies" who see them on the streets, pick them up, clean them off, clothe them in finery, give them tasty food to eat, and then offer to bring them to a good place, an Islahaya. The sad truth is that "nice ladies" don't exist, never do they pick up these dirty children, clean them, give them adequate food and clothing, nor do they bring them to places of refuge. Rather, "nice ladies" steer clear of grubby begging hands and ragged bodies. Yet, when the Islahaya girls initially tell their stories, they exaggerate and often lie, to create an aura around their captivity, fashioning some of the most wondrous Egyptian versions of Cinderella stories imaginable. By exaggerating, the girls clothe themselves in invisible armour; their womb-like semi-reality makes the harsh reality of their existence more tolerable.

****

Samira's story as told to Nevien in 2011:

Samira, can you tell us your story?

My parents put me in the car, drove somewhere in the city and just pushed me out. I have never seen them or heard from them since then.

How old are you now Samira?

What year is this?

It's 2011.

I think I remember being told I was born in 1994 so that would make me how old?

You'd be seventeen now. Do you remember how old you were or how long ago when your parents left you?

I've been here for about six years and I think I was on the streets for about two years, so I guess how old would I have been?

That would make you nine when your parents threw you out. Do you know why they did this to you?

In tears, Samira mentions a new baby brother and several other children. *My mother just had a new baby and he was my baby brother, I also had other brothers and I think one sister. We had to sleep in one bed, and I guess there was no room for me.*

Samira, can you tell us what happened when you were on the streets by yourself?

Hesitantly, Samira recounts, *I was really scared, and hungry. I didn't have any money or even any clothes, I remember getting really cold at night because I didn't have a jacket. I just begged for food, for money, all I wanted was to go home.*

And then...

I saw a policeman, I couldn't read, but I know the uniform. I begged him for help, he just pushed me away and laughed. Finally I went to what I was sure was a police station. They laughed at me, but beat me first, then threw me out. I remember them telling me not to bother them anymore. I just wanted them to help me but they wouldn't. I found scraps of food behind McDonald's and Burger King, so I ate this just because I was so hungry. I had to fight with the cats who kept trying to take my food from me.

Did you meet with any girls your own age on the streets?

After a while I did. We all stayed together. One day we were all caught by the police, maybe they didn't like us because we were all together. Anyway, they brought us to the station, took our pictures, asked a lot of questions about who we were, our names and things like that. I couldn't tell them anything except my name is Samira. They wrote everything down and brought us here to this Islahaya.

Are all the girls still here who were locked up with you?

No, I'm the only one. We were all locked in these small rooms for a long time, and the supervisors gave us some food, but we couldn't talk to each other and then finally they let me out, but the other girls were gone. I've never seen them again.

Samira is just one of the thousands who was deserted by her family, left to survive or not on the streets, picked up by police and eventually brought,

with a police record attached to her, to the Islahaya.

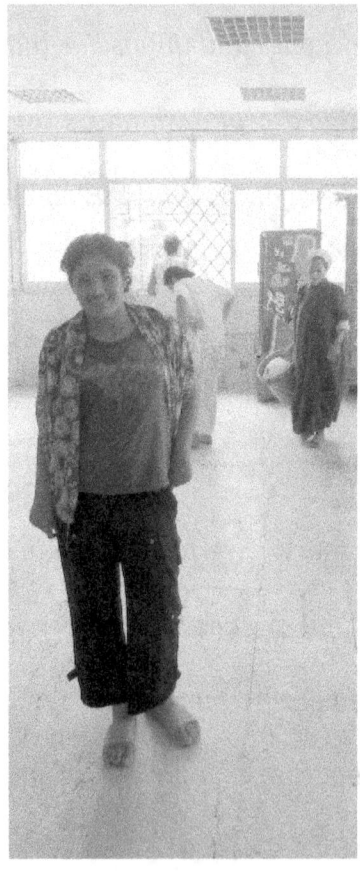

Samira in 2011

****

Wafaa isn't quite sure, but thinks she's ten. How she came to the Islahaya in about 2009 is beyond her young memory. Her life now consists of bars and gates, dirty walls, a thin mattress on a makeshift bed. But for Wafaa, this is much better than the streets; at least she gets meals of foul (beans), rice, and Arabic bread. Rather than being one of the thousands wandering the streets, her community is now around a hundred girls with some sort of routine. But then, what of the rest of her life? At ten, Wafaa's life should be about beginnings, but at ten in the Islahaya, it's about nothing, about endings, about no in-between. Wafaa gave the same story of the "nice lady" who helped her to find the Agouza Islahaya. Yet, the "nice lady" is not a lady at all, but the girls' metaphor for police who bring these unfortunate children to their stations. So at ten, her life will never be the same, picked up by the police, brought to the Islahaya, there to spend the rest of her life, or at least until she's old enough to go back on the streets to

prostitution, begging, or crime.

Wafaa in 2011

****

The government somewhere realizes these institutions exist, but acknowledgment means action, so in the case of these girls, the authorities turn a blind eye to the situation of the girls. The government keeps records, somewhere, in some very archaic fashion, and apparently the madams know their own accountability. Yet from first-hand experience, sitting in the office, listening to their discussions over funds and disbursements, it's easy to see how these women get away with doctoring the records. My Arabic is good enough to know that in any language, they engage in doublespeak, with great courtesy, but nonetheless, doublespeak. So it doesn't take great deductive powers to know there is no very strict accounting of which funds go for the girls and which funds go elsewhere.

The principle is simple, more girls, and more money which mysteriously disappears. Where does government money go? It's anyone's guess. Certainly it isn't spent on the girls, clothes, or necessities.

Poverty plagues Egypt; education is equated with wealth, even though government schools exist in the cities and country towns, these are only for children with families, names, identities. In addition, the quality of these schools is limited. This quality can only be judged by the abilities and preparedness of its teachers and the dedication to the idea of education by a country's population at large. This appears to be one of the most important hurdles which must be overcome. Even in the state schools, the cost for parents to send their children to school is more than many can afford. School uniforms, supplies, transportation to and from school, all these add up. Egyptian families have so many children that many cannot afford to send all their children to school. It's not unusual to see gangs of children wandering the streets during school hours, children who have homes and families, not street children with no one. Parents don't always keep track of their children's whereabouts during the day and as Egypt is a very late-night culture, this may carry on till very late hours. Education is secondary to survival, and mothers in particular are so busy working, often as cleaners, and then caring for husbands and other family members, that knowing if children are attending school is not always done.

A further serious problem in addition to teacher preparedness, and parental oversight, is salary for the teachers. When a government teacher's salary begins at £300 Egyptian per month, equivalent of less than 60US, what quality of education is delivered? What incentive drives any Egyptian fortunate enough to attend university and select the field of education knowing that income is rock-bottom and working conditions abysmal? With little or no inducement to provide quality education, it is not surprising that the academic level of most government teachers cannot begin to be favourable. Less surprising then is the quality or qualifications of the teacher assigned to Islahaya education to provide any sort of education for these girls.

Egypt's street girls become *IL Binait Dol* or *Those Girls*, those street children convicted, sentenced, and punished in the most insensible way possible, thrown out of society into the world of Islahaya. What real crimes have these young girls committed?

****

Samia does not remember her natural father, only the step-father who came into her life when she was eight. Pretty, young, and sweet, these qualities attracted the man in his thirties who lusted after the young child. He got his way; her mother offered no protection, a common practice among poor families, and sometimes in wealthy families. In all these families, a young girl must learn to take it or be beaten, sometimes beaten in any event.

Samia ran away, became lost in Cairo's alleyways and soon found kindred spirits, young girls who suffered the same abuse. But their problems were only beginning. With no protection and no place to go, Samia and her new 'family' were swooped up by a gang of older boys who offered them food in exchange for the same services from which they ran away. If they chose not to go along with the gang sex, the choice was to selling boxes of tissues to passers-by, endangering their lives, stepping into traffic, begging drivers, passengers, anyone, to buy their tissues. If they didn't reach their quota of selling, gang leaders beat them and use them for sex anyway.

Samia was one of the lucky girls, the police picked her up early in her street career, brought her to the station, and when she had no family name or information to give, branded her a criminal and brought her to the Islahaya. Samia's street friend Noor suffered the same fate, but Noor endured something else from the police in addition to brutal treatment as a street girl. Two of the police raped her first then branded her a criminal before bringing her to the Islahaya. Noor was eleven, a more attractive conquest than the younger Samia.

After living in the Islahaya for two years, the desperation and pain of life within its walls became too much for Samia, she began cutting herself. She continues this practice even though the supervisors punish them severely for self-mutilation. Samia's fate is no different from the other girls, eventually she will be thrust out of the Islahaya, a life she despises, to one on the streets. The self-inflicted pain helps her deal with the uncertainty which awaits her.

****

Nadia's story:

She told my students (in 2006) that in return for sex, the guard sometimes let her outside where she roams at night with some of her old gang. Sometimes she steals to buy food, cigarettes, or sweets, other times she sleeps with men for a few piasters (cents). She always returned to the Islahaya during the day, played the role of a model Islahaya girl thereby earning the privilege of classroom education. This was the only way she came in contact with my students from AUC.

Nadia said she had sex with many boys before being caught. She never had to sell street items, just herself. She talked about the pain of sex because as a young girl from Upper Egypt, she remembers being cut [FGM or Female Genital Mutilation]. Below is her remembrance.

I remember an older woman holding me down while another cut into my 'private parts'. All I remember then is blood streaming between my legs. Then the old woman sewed me up and left a small hole just big enough for me to use the toilet.

When my mother remarried, we came to Cairo and that's when I ran away. My step-father used to beat me all the time and I couldn't take it anymore. Then I met up with those boys and they wanted to have sex with me. It hurt so much, it was worse at first, and then I got used to the pain. Pain helps, you don't think about anything else. So I cut myself sometimes too, that helps me forget my life.

But I do other things that the supervisors like so now they let me come to classes. I want to learn, maybe one day I can get out.

She wants more than anything to leave and begin a real life, but has no actual plan of how to get out. As of 2011, Nadia still resides in the Islahaya, getting close to the age and time when she too will be cast out onto the streets.

Nadia 2011

****

Do the madams or keepers feel remorse at the treatment they give to the girls? They rationalize that the only way to keep the girls behaving is to cut them off from society, because they are not worthy to be out in the world anyway, to punish them severely, to banish them from education, even as sparse as it is inside the Islahaya, and to forbid them normal pleasures. What the girls do have inside is the guarantee of three meals a day, mostly consisting of foul, rice, an occasional piece of meat, for one of the three meals, and a place which is not on the street. Can the girls be raped on the inside? Most assuredly, rape is a part of what they have come to expect, but the rape within the Islahaya, comes from some of the other girls who have formed tough gangs. If caught, these gang members receive punishment, but often the keepers fear retaliation from these girls. Therefore, they are usually not punished, and the rapes continue. Rape is not a new concept for these young girls, nor is dominance from older women alien to any of them.

****

In discussions of gender discrimination between Egyptian men and women, my students often declared that mothers are the dominant members of a household, even over the husbands. The students engaged in many lively debates, often very divided between the female and male students over this issue. Many conclusions were reached; they began to realize the cultural differences between Western gender theory and disparate gender roles within a Middle Eastern culture such as their own. But one point emerged throughout, that although the woman may in many cases wield a dominant voice within the household, the father or eldest male commanded the final voice. To this end, the students began to understand why step-mothers and even mothers from these dysfunctional families strove to achieve authority within the home.

****

Maitha, a young mother of about twenty-seven, brought her two infant girls to the Islahaya. When I first saw Maitha, I thought she must have been about fifty. She had no teeth, her withered skin shrivelled against a skeletal face; she couldn't stand straight, most likely due to malnutrition. Maitha had in tow her two very young daughters, one about two and the other four. She had only come for a day to visit the children, but had to leave them behind as her husband had deserted her and the girls leaving her with no means of support. We couldn't discover where Maitha's lived after she left the Islahaya. Her daughters clung to their mother's hands as she walked out and away from them. Maitha wouldn't allow pictures of herself but here are her daughters, branded and labelled – Cairo's youngest criminals?

Cairo's youngest criminals – Maitha's daughters

****

In the Islahaya, discussions and supplies for personal hygiene don't really take place. The girls don't have regular washing routines, nor do they have the facilities or equipment, i.e. toothbrushes, toothpaste, shampoo, etc for daily care. Those topics and supplies are left to a few occasional volunteers – they take it upon themselves to bring shampoo and other necessary items to the girls. These items cannot be given to the supervisors as the items never get to the girls, but disappear into the pockets of the supervisors.

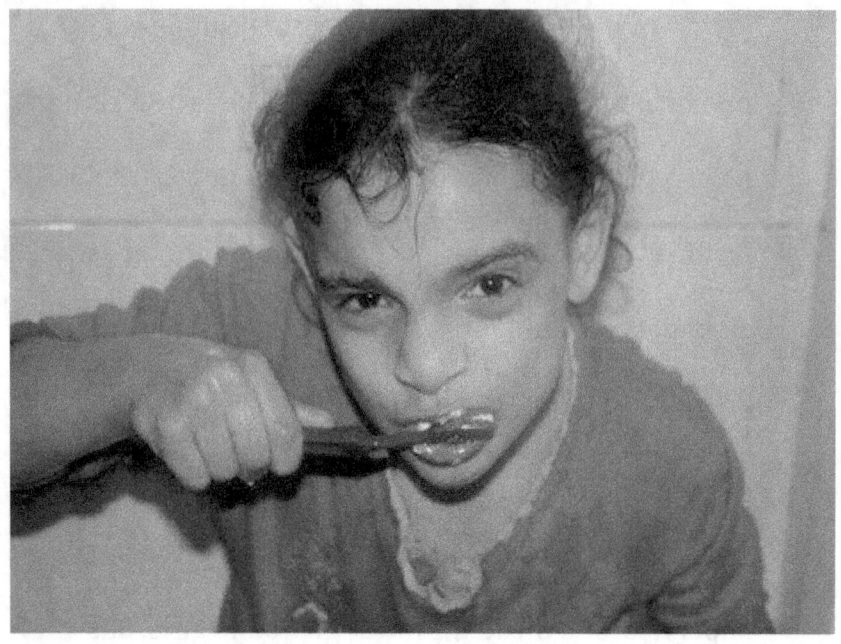

Learning from the volunteers how to brush her teeth

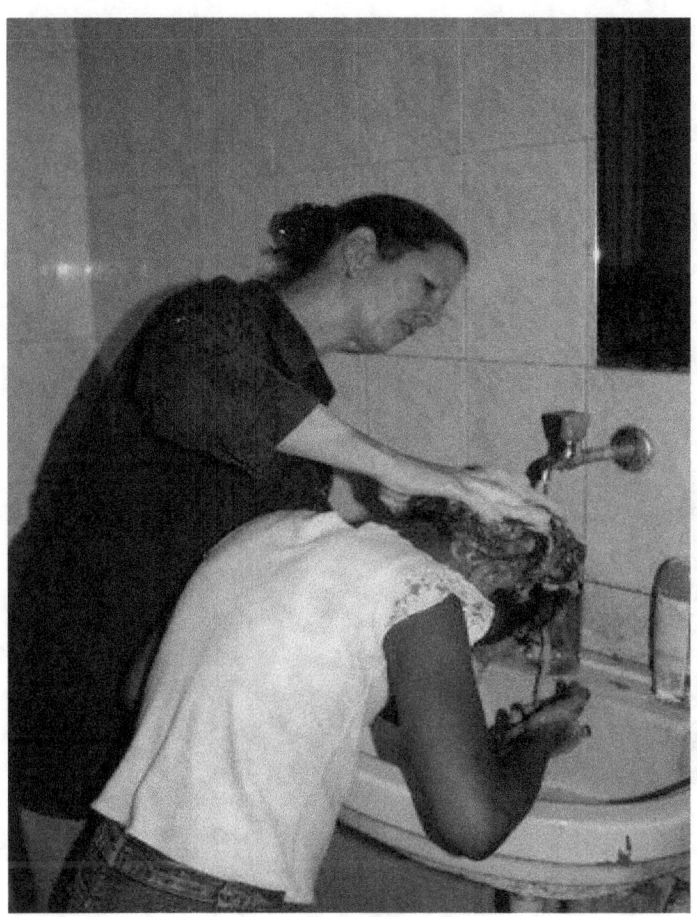

A DEO volunteer giving a good wash with lice shampoo

Happy to be clean – happy that someone cares

Other intimate topics such as sexuality, what it is,

and how the body functions, do not take place within

the Islahaya. Teachers don't take this upon themselves

to discuss these things with the girls; the government

discourages openness on this subject, so the girls learn

what they can, usually in the roughest manner. So when the older and tougher girls form a rape gang or sneak into the beds of other girls for sexual relations, the younger more vulnerable don't fight. To them, it's human touch, although many girls are too young to understand what is happening to them. Of course in Islam, this is *haram* or forbidden, but for them human touch in any form is what they need.

As we get closer to the lives of these children, it is vital to grasp the vast array of problems surrounding these girls. Not merely runaways who leave lovely homes in fits of anger, *Il Binait Dol* cry out to become real persons, to have real lives, to be respected members of a society which either out of embarrassment or fear chooses to ignore or put aside their very existence. They deserve the world's attention; they have a right to the humanity which claims every intelligent person's moral discretion.

Branded criminals – three young Il Binait Dol – "Those Girls"

Chapter Four

Outside the Walls

Four-year-old Zeinab's parents deserted her in the middle of Cairo's streets, shoved her away, walked in a different direction and never looked back. That was about fifty-two years ago. Picked up almost immediately by the police, Zeinab could not answer their questions. She had no ability to speak, and within a short space of time it became quite obvious that Zeinab was not "normal." The police could not discover anything about her, not even her name, so they gave her one, Zeinab, booked her as a criminal as required by law, and brought her to the Islahaya in Agouza where to this day she still resides. She doesn't really speak, she can say good morning and a few basic phrases, but that is the extent of her language skills.

Zeinab and three Islahaya girls

Zeinab's story, tragic in her abandonment, tells

us that Islahayas existed in the middle of the twentieth

century. When Zeinab entered, chaos ruled the

Islahaya, records were incomplete, children like Zeinab-obviously mentally challenged -and others -street children abandoned, runaways, and petty thieves-were bundled together in a human lump. No care was taken or given to the children as to their needs, physical, sociological, or educational. Considered as anathema to society, the children needed confinement, secured away from public view. Shunted off immediately to an Islahaya, Zeinab was most likely spared the other horrors of life to which abandoned children are subjected. She has been a resident inmate for at least fifty-two years. For her, retarded, very young, and alone, the Islahaya offered some form of protection and it's the only home she's really ever known.

For girls roaming Cairo's streets life outside the Islahaya walls is rough, tough, lonely, and terrible. Street survival in Cairo requires hardening of emotions; otherwise a child becomes fodder for anyone to abuse and use.

Typical Egyptian street scene – easy to get lost and hide from authorities

Life on the streets: a vendor selling his wares

****

Noor's Story:

I think I'm now sixteen. I ran away from home

about six years ago, the madams tell me the year I came

here was 2008, so I guess I ran away in 2007.

Noor, why did you run away?

I ran away because my mother's husband beat me and his son raped me. I kept trying to complain but every time I did my step-father beat me some more. Every day he beat me, he said I needed to stop lying, stop accusing his son of raping me. Finally I couldn't take it anymore, so I got up in the middle of the night, put some things in a plastic bag and ran away. I wanted to come to Cairo, but I didn't know how far it was.

Do you know where your family lives?

We had a very small piece of land in a village near Saqqara. There was nothing there except some watermelons, cucumbers, and tomatoes which we grew to sell at market. I didn't mind working in the fields, but every night I just couldn't take the beatings or being raped. I knew Cairo would be a better place to live.

But when I got to Cairo, everything was frightening. I had no money, I didn't know anyone, and I didn't know where to go. I was so tired too, I had walked almost the whole way to the city. For the first few days, I ate food I found on the streets, slept in my plastic bag, wrapping it around me to keep warm. I remember once I found a piaster on the ground, I bought some sweets. I had to keep moving around. I recognized police and they scared me. After a few days I met some other kids from the streets. They let me stay with them and gave me some food to eat, but they said I would have to work for more food and a place to sleep if I wanted to stay with them.

Do you know how many were in the gang? Were there boys and girls? Did you trust them? What did they ask you to do?

There were about maybe fifteen, maybe more. They gave me small boxes of tissues to sell, and sometimes

I sold lemons or mint bunches to tourists. But if I didn't sell enough, the older boys wouldn't give me any food, but they still let me sleep in the empty house where they stayed. Whenever I sold things, all the money had to go to the older boys. If they thought I stole, they would beat me. One boy I knew kept some money and they beat him so badly I don't know if he died. That frightened me, so I never stole any money.

I don't know where the older boys got the things to sell, I just know I had to do my job, make my quota, and not betray where we lived to anyone outside the gang. After a little while, I don't really know how long, a few of the older boys became very friendly with me.

What do you mean friendly?

They would come into my mattress at night. It felt like love, sometimes they would sleep with me, but it wasn't like my step-brother, they didn't hurt me. I began to like this attention. Soon the others, mostly the girls in the gang, showed me respect, even though I was one of the youngest there. I got the job of teaching the newest members how to beg, how to sell, and mostly the rules of living in the group.

One night some strangers came to our sleeping place. They argued with a couple of other boys, beat them, and I became really afraid for the first time. I didn't know who they were or what they wanted. They looked all of us girls over and without warning, one of them took me. It was like before, like being with my step-brother. He hurt me, tied my arms down and just kept on forcing himself on me.

What did you do then?

That's when I ran away. I thought I could live by myself again on the streets, I knew what to do, where I was. But the police grabbed me, brought me to a station, threw me in a back room with dirty floors and no one

around but a lot of dirty, smelly men. For a long time, the

police asked me questions, I refused to tell them anything,

there were three other girls in the room with me, we

didn't answer the police. They didn't feed us, they

wouldn't let us use the toilet, and one of the men beat us

to make us talk. We began to make up stories, but we

never told them where our friends were. Finally, they took

our pictures, our names, and then drove us to the

Islahaya where I still live. The other girls left here – I

never knew their names and I don't know where they

went.

Isn't it better in the Islahaya? You don't have to

sell on the streets or worry about beatings.

It's as bad here as at home, if we don't do

everything they say, the madams do beat us, take away

our food, and don't let us go to classes. Two times I

escaped.

How did you escape?

That I won't tell you. But the police caught me

almost right away and brought me back here. Madam

Ibtisam, the director, locked me in a small cupboard for

two days, I think. I hate it here; I hate the directors and

everything about this place. It smells, the other girls are

bullies; the only good thing is tricking the directors that

I'm good so they let me go to Madam Hanna's teachers. I

hate being in the Islahaya, I can't run free. Madam

Ibtisam locks me when I say some bad words; and they

chain me to my bed. I had to use a bucket for the toilet

and then clean it up myself.

What will you do? Stay here or try to escape

again?

I will escape, but the right way, I will learn how to read and write, maybe get out that way, somehow. I have to get out; I just have to get out.

That was the end of her story, she wouldn't tell us more, not about any of the other girls – it's as if she suddenly became afraid she's disclosed too much already.

Noor 2012

****

Most of the girls come from towns away from Cairo, usually near the Nile where poor families live on subsistence farming. The areas are poor, untidy, the Nile tributaries snake up to give moisture to the bits of farmland used to raise mostly tomatoes, cucumbers, and other vegetables to sell at market. In the Nile animals bathe next to spots where women wash clothes and tin pots, dishes and drinking cups. Villagers use the river for drinking water, dumping waste, and watering their crops. Heavy fertilizers must be used as the river no longer has the rich silt since the building of Aswan in the 1950s.

Carcass in the Nile next to home use

Carcasses of dead animals float by on occasion, adding to the general murkiness of the water. Life is difficult, a bare subsistence. Farming methods are primitive, by hand and oxen only, no modern equipment or machinery is used to cultivate the land. Families tend to bond together in these small villages. Intermarriage is expected, relationships are so interconnected that it's difficult to draw any line separating the various families.

Typical Nile River scene, animals, food, water, washing, all use the same water

****

As told to Nevien in 2012:

My name is Wafaa and I just want to leave this place. What did I do, why didn't my father keep me, why didn't he send my other sister or brothers away?

Wafaa, tell us what happened to you.

My mother died I think it was about when I was eight, that was a long time ago, they tell me I'm now fifteen, and this is 2012, but I'm not sure. I know I was the baby in the family. I have five brothers and one sister and one day my father just put us all in his old car, and stuffed one large plastic bag with clothes inside. I thought we were going to visit someone in the family, but instead, he drove to a very busy street, opened the back door, and one of my brothers threw the bag out and then pushed me on to the ground, then they all drove off.

What did you think happened? What did you do?

I didn't know what to do, I just sat there on the ground crying, please come back! But he never did, I have never seen my father or family ever again. I was at the gate of this place, this Islahaya and the guard at the gate came and brought me inside. He gave my bag of clothes to the madam, I've never seen those things again either.

Then what happened?

Before I knew anything else the police came and took me away. They said I had to have papers before I could live in the Islahaya.

Did they tell you what kind of papers?

They didn't say much, just took me in a room in their station, took my picture and then said 'you're a criminal'. I didn't even know what a criminal was, how could I be one, I'm an Egyptian!

What did they do next?

They brought me back here. I kept asking, 'what have I done?' I didn't understand then and I still don't. I couldn't tell the police much, I never knew my father's name, or where we lived, I'm not really sure how old I am.

But they made stuff up, took my picture, and then brought

me back to the Islahaya.

Wafaa, what happened next?

I cried every night and almost every day. I am

small for my age, the older girls picked on me, and at

night they climbed into my mattress and forced things on

me. Sometimes it was a piece of wood, or other things and

put them inside me, making me have sex with them. I

hated what they did, I hated them, but I had no one to

talk to, I couldn't complain. Whenever I cried the

supervisors beat me, they didn't want any complaints, so I

had to lie there and take it.

Did it ever get easier or better?

It wasn't any easier during the day. The big girls

would sneak behind me; hit me and then run away,

laughing. I couldn't talk to the supervisors then either. All

I wanted to do was run away. But how? So I did,

eventually, and no I won't tell you how, that's something

we can never do here.

Why can't you tell us how you escaped or where
you went?

If we escape, it's a promise not to tell so that

others might have the same chance if they want. I learned

quickly, there were some girls I could talk to, they didn't

like the big girls either. It took me a long time, but I

finally learned a trick to leave this place. Please don't ask

how, but I can tell you that the supervisors are not always

careful about checking our beds at night.

What did you do when you left? Do you know
how old you were? Where did you go?

I had no money, no place to go, and no place to

sleep but I didn't care. It was in the middle of the night, it

was freedom. I think I was maybe nine when I ran away.

What happened next, do you remember?

I slept behind buildings, sometimes even in dumpsters where I could also find food scraps. It wasn't long before I met other kids like me, but they were together usually in groups. They invited me to go with them and that's when I became part of their gang. But there were some older boys in the gang and they frightened me, so I ran away from them too.

How long were you on the streets – and were you always by yourself?

I stayed on the streets for a long time, I even remember during one Ramadan and for a month I got food at the street tables.

What were you doing during the days?

I went looking for my family, I walked through all kinds of neighbourhoods, but I never found any place that looked like my home. I just wanted to find my father and

brothers, I didn't want the police to catch me, so I would

hide out whenever I saw a policeman. Sometimes I got

lucky and found money someone lost, then I knew I could

eat for a couple of days, but mostly I just walked and

walked, looking for my family.

Did you ever meet someone who helped you in all that time?

Yes, one day I was walking near Tahrir Square

and met this old woman who sold sweets to the university

students. She sat right on the pavement, set out her

sweets and stayed there all day. I sat down beside her and

she talked to me in such a nice way and then when she

needed help, I did things for her. She slept right under the

front gate at the university and had enough room for me,

so when she invited me to stay with her, I did. It was like

having a grandmother.[19]

How long did you stay with her?

I'm not sure, but I know that it was through a hot

summer, a Ramadan, and a cold winter. She was really

kind to me, the students and others weren't always very

nice, but sometimes they'd put money in her box without

taking any sweets, so we usually had enough money to

buy something to eat.

Then eventually the police caught you?

Yes, they found me one day, I was going to the

corner McDonald's to buy us a real meal when they saw

me. They picked me up, put me in the police van – what

was terrible, they didn't even let me bring food to my

---

[19] These eaves were located just outside the guardhouse to the university entrance, but the guards turned a blind eye to the old woman's "tenement" out of kindness to her age, inability to live elsewhere, and because she never annoyed anyone.

friend or bring back her money, they just brought me to a

station and then I guess they had my picture because they

drove me back to this Islahaya. I've never seen her again,

I feel very bad, can you bring a message to her for me?

We will try to let her know about you if she's still there. (We did make the attempt, but by this time the university had moved to the desert and the old woman who lived under the eaves had disappeared.)

Wafaa, what do you want to do now?

I am trying to stay good, not run away; because that's the only way I can take classes from Madam Hanna's teachers, Hala and Wafaa. If I can learn to read and write, and maybe take the exams, then maybe I won't be beaten any more by the supervisors and then I can leave here. I'd like to get a job, and go to school. What I really want is to be a doctor!

Wafaa is now taking classes, but her chances of getting employment or a further education are slim to none. She has no name, no legal standing in the community and there is no way she can be accepted at a university with her lack of credentials; she's from the Islahaya and has a criminal record. But it is cruel to tell her these things, it's so much better to let her hope and perhaps that hope can become a reality.

****

Today, Zeinab, the oldest resident, has freedom of movement within the institution. The directors have no fear she will run away, institutionalized, severely handicapped she has no place to run, no ability to plan an escape, nor any desire or thought of leaving. She sits at the front gate on the stone wall day in and day out, welcoming visitors although her speaking ability is very limited. You see her just sitting, sometimes watching the birds, often watching as people pass. I wondered many times what she thought, if anything. Does she understand life on the outside in any fashion? She was only four when her family left her at the entrance. She loves to partake in all the activities, wishes to help with the younger ones in washing their hair, eat cakes and drink juice when offered, and pose for photographs. She is completely illiterate, no attempt has ever been made to educate her, she is incapable of craft work taught to some of the other girls, has absolutely no outside contacts, no family or friends. Her life died when her parents dumped her at the Islahaya gates more than fifty years ago.

Wafaa on the other hand looks forward to continuing her education. Finally realizing the importance of completing her studies and taking the *Adadaya*, getting legal identity papers without which the girls are doomed to an imprisoned life. Wafaa would love to be a doctor. But to do this she must attend high school first, pass her *Thanawa*,[20] get a place at University, and then hope for the impossible, find someone to assist her outside while she attends University. This entails funding her studies, personal expenses, and most importantly, finding and paying for room and board during her attendance at University. This is her dream and some way must be found for Wafaa and other girls like her to become working and respected members of Egyptian society. A first step toward achieving this goal would be to properly administer the money made available for the Islahaya by the government.

What about Noor's ambitions and fate. Noor too finally realized the importance of education through the DEO teachers. Initially more violent than Wafaa, Noor

---

[20] The *Thanawa* is the high school exam after completing the full spectrum of high school courses and must be passed in order to gain entry in to any university or college.

had much to overcome. She also had to break all ties with her gang members on the outside; she did sneak out twice more, but if she tries again, she will be sent away. More than two escapes results in severe punishment, removal of privileges, ban on attending school, no outings and possibly sent to an Islahaya distant from Cairo. Properly chastened Noor has in mind to take the *Adadaya*, but after that she has little ambition except marriage. During one of her escapes, she began a relationship with one of the boys in her old gang. If this relationship lasts, and if he can earn money enough for their marriage, then this might be possible. However, he too is a street child, although no longer a child, his skills and literacy are nonexistent. What can he do, how can he succeed in life for himself, let alone assume family responsibilities? Noor will have some education, just beyond functional literacy, but are these skills enough to assist in a marriage that has little foundation except the personal element?

Il Binait Dol tend not to speak about the future, it's their Goliath, their fear, the insurmountable. They merely hope and wish for a bright light to shine on them bringing mercy and any help it can. On the outside, girls are raped, sell themselves in prostitution. The obvious question arises, what about pregnancies? Do the girls–babies most of them–have babies themselves?

Pregnancies are all too common among these girls when they leave or escape the Islahaya; they have babies and of course cannot care for them. The options are illegal abortions of which many occur but this too is *haram* in the Arab world; have the baby and if it's a boy, deposit it at an orphanage, if a girl, dump the infant in dumpsters to die. If a girl is on the street, the boy may marry her and that too is an option, but like one girl from the Islahaya who escaped, became pregnant, and

eventually turned herself back in to the Islahaya but the

directors in Agouza do not keep these girls. Their babies

may be sold, left to die, or brought to orphanages;[21] it's

a very gray area, very murky waters into which it's

difficult to wade.

How many Islahayas exist in Egypt or in Cairo?

Members of the Ministry of Social Affairs have not

responded to this enquiry or any others put to them

regarding Islahayas. Similar to Hanna's failed attempts

to bring the girls to Ras Sudr since 2011, the Ministry

officials either say one thing and do exactly the opposite

or else they refuse to speak at all. It is unclear whether

this is due to ignorance about the workings of the

Islahayas in general, or to their reluctance to let out this

---

[21] Adoption is essentially illegal in the Islamic culture. A child must have a father's name and identity, so these "dumped" babies may be brought to an orphanage, and if fortunate, to one which educates its children, but they cannot go to a family; the orphanage becomes their family.

information about this terrible, darkly kept hidden shame.

It was very difficult for the girls to share their stories and a collective thanks is given for bringing us into their lives.

Chapter Five

Law, Marriage, and the Family

Marriage and family, family and marriage are the watchwords of Egyptian girls from earliest childhood. Family life in the Middle East means everything. Though it can easily be argued that family means much in many cultures, in Arab society family endows every member with identity, self-respect, and validation as a member of country, neighbourhoods, with all the privileges of this membership. Those without this family identity are considered incomplete.

A former student of mine, one who took part in the Gender course and spent time working with the girls in the Islahaya, has herself struggled with family issues. Although only her father is Egyptian, my student was born and raised in Egypt. For many years, she grappled with the problems besetting her within a culture that preached control of women through various means, if not legally, then through guilt and family pressure. She strove to find her own identity within this complex culture of male dominance. She once wrote,

> *I need to break the news to my father that I'm just not going to stay in Egypt to let him be happy. I think it's selfish of him and my uncle to want to keep me there because it makes them feel comfortable. I think I'm entitled to a life. And I'm not going to find one in Egypt. I don't want to just get married and have children and sit there. Work opportunities are mediocre and the pay is terrible, I'm too old to be living with my parents and I would really like a sense of self accomplishment.*

Sara is fortunate in that she has the means for self-support, education, and the ability to change her life. In sharp contrast the Islahaya girls, street girls, cannot go outside and make a life. They do not have the luxury of choice.

Anyone unfamiliar with the deep-seated family "layers" in Arab cultures might misunderstand and attempt to equate these familial relationships with family values in the West. This can be explained in an incident which occurred in the city of Alexandria – the destruction of a Coptic church by irate family members.

This incident, as reported in international news, omitted certain details. It began and ended as a family affair. A young man and woman, one a Christian, the other a Muslim, had a relationship and wished to marry. This created a family uproar on both sides. But the father of the young Muslim approached the other family and they agreed to settle their differences and allow the young people to marry. Uncles and cousins of this young man were so irate and angered by the father's decision that they took it upon themselves in reckless disregard for anyone's safety to destroy the Alexandria church where the Christian family prayed, even to the destruction of a place of worship demonstrates the strength of family unity.

****

Nelly's story – an AUC student as told to me in 2007:

Nelly had been missing classes and after repeated attempts to reach her, she finally came to my office with her story.

My mother just died two weeks ago and I have had the responsibility for all the arrangements and sat with her every day until she died.

You could have applied for a leave from this semester and picked up again next year, Nelly.

I just didn't think about it and there's another problem. I have a fiancé and we have both been taking classes to convert to Christianity.

Why is this a problem? Did your mother know?

My mother knew and supported me the whole way, but if my father, my uncles, cousins, or my grandmother find out they will beat me first, then send me away and stop paying for my university. My mother was my only support, she even wrote a letter before she died, but I am really afraid to give it to my father.

What about your fiancé's family? Are they supportive?

Nobody knows, we have to keep it very secret. We just want to get married and set up our own place first, I need to finish my degree, I only have two semesters left, and then we can tell our families. If they even get a hint of us converting, both families will come down on us and take away any inheritance.

Will you be able to do all this without your family knowing?

I hope so, but you know how it is here, family is everything, it comes first, even before what we need. My father is sometimes a bully and he won't listen, so I have to make sure everything is set before they know about our conversion.

Nelly and her fiancé managed to get everything arranged, the family never found out about their religious conversion until a year after they married. By that time, her father had mellowed, read his wife's dying request that he accept his daughter's decisions and both families agree to disagree. But Nelly had education, her mother's support and a fiancé who made the same choices. This example, though, shows the strength of family, immediate and extended in Middle Eastern countries. It brings into sharp contrast the isolation of the street girls with no support at their backs. As of 2012, Nelly and her husband still lived and worked in Cairo with family support on all sides.

****

Marriage generally consists of three stages, but it is the first stage, the contract and of what it consists that demonstrates Arab, Muslim, and in this case Egyptian customs. The contract concerns the woman, not only what she will bring to the marriage, but what, in the event of divorce, she gets out of the relationship. Whether it's children, money, furniture, dowry, cars, flat, or house, these items must be included in the contract. Another necessary article for inclusion is if the woman will have the right to ask for a divorce or as some word the contract that divorce will be in the woman's hands, her decision, her choice. Regardless of verbal promises made prior to marriage, everything must be in the contract; otherwise, it will be virtually impossible for a woman to take out of a marriage what is hers.

These contracts called *Katb al Kitab* play a vital role in the future of the marriage, the man and woman individually, and in any family disputes or allegiances. One of my former colleagues shared her experience with the *Katb al Kitab*. Sherine's family insisted that the matter of divorce, if it came up, would rest solely in her hands and be her decision. He, the prospective bridegroom, did not agree but as his family anxiously wished for the marriage, they agreed to everything, overriding their son's wishes. In the end, Sherine called off the wedding. She did not really trust her fiancé and did not want a life bound to a man who attempted to control her every move. Fortunately for her, her parents supported her decision. Yet her former fiancé and his family still pursue her relentlessly to no avail. Unlike the Islahaya girls, she has many options to stay away from him, education, travel, and family support.

Another form of marriage which men will use on unsuspecting women is called an *arfy* marriage. Under *Shari'a* law it is *haram* for a man to have sexual relations with a woman unless she is his wife. This goes without saying for a woman, but the *arfy* marriage is a way around these restrictions for a man. In Egypt, a man can be arrested for spending the night with a woman not his wife. However, a man may write an agreement between him and the woman he wishes to be with. The agreement contains whatever the man wishes to include such as rights to her bank account, property, possessions. Only the man can tear up the agreement. In the eyes of the law, they are a married couple. Some men use this type of "marriage" with foreign women, many of whom have suffered as a result. She cannot tear up the agreement; the law recognizes only his authority. I personally know several women, expatriates in Egypt, who have lost everything, bank accounts, cars, furniture when an *arfy* husband decides to divorce. Yet foreign women are not the only victims of such a marriage.

****

Rehab's mother had such a marriage, the result of which drastically affected her children, Rehab and a younger brother. After her mother and father died, within months of each other, Rehab's brother brought her to the Islahaya; according to her story he brought her to the Islahaya to avoid problems—there were beatings by relatives and Rehab was raped by a cousin.

Her brother couldn't protect her so they ran away to Cairo where he now lives on the street while she is imprisoned in the Islahaya.

This was some of the story, but one of the supervisors there, Madam Nehad,[22] painted a much bleaker picture. The real situation was that her mother got married to an Egyptian from Aswan, but it was only an *arfy* marriage. When this man died, her mother took the children to Sharkia – a Delta governorate in Lower Egypt. Shortly after the mother died the family with whom the children lived, denied that they were legal children. They did not want them to have part of their mother's inheritance. The children had no birth certificates or papers, even though secular law clearly states that a DNA test can be performed to prove that

---

[22] It must be explained that Madame Nehad, one of the junior directors of the Agouza Islahaya, is also one of the few who really cares about the girls, but in general is powerless to help in any way except to listen to their stories.

arfy children are legally from the mother. The brother works occasionally in a juice stand and the rest of the time roams Cairo's streets with other homeless youths. This tragedy began three years ago; Rehab wants to get out, is often rebellious and beaten, in particular by Madam Naglaa, the afternoon director. Rehab is uncertain of her age—she thinks she's about twenty-- and has been in the Islahaya for over three years, is still uneducated, and all she sees of life is a dark hole with no way out.

In Rehab's situation, her mother's entire family became involved. Uncles and aunts who wanted to inherit her mother's possessions and money, a cousin who raped her, an unconcerned and uncaring family for this young girl. The *arfy* marriage offered no protection for the children. Though recognized in the courts, the family made sure that the children, Rehab and her brother, were disinherited. Had the father survived the mother, then he would have a legal claim on his "wife's" possessions, leaving the children out if he chose. Fortunately for them, they did not have to find out as their father died just before the mother. In this situation, the children have a law protecting their interests; but to whom can they turn for help? Illiterate, friendless, and strangers in Cairo, the problem lays in that there is little to no recourse for these or other similarly placed children.

Rehab still incarcerated - 2011

****

Passent at nineteen has been in the Islahaya since 2008. Her parents divorced, mother remarried, and while living with her step-father who beat and raped her, she ran away to live in the streets. She slept near mosques by night, stole and begged by day.

Passent uses the "nice lady" version of getting to the

Islahaya, but in fact Madame Nehad explained that the

police brought her in. The director was happy to have

Passent speak with us because she likes living in the

Islahaya, and does not wish to return to the streets.

What she really wishes is to complete her education and

become a doctor. After her *Adadaya,* she wants to

attend high school and pass the *Thanawa* or high school

exams. Unfortunately, there is little chance for this as

Hanna must pay for anything beyond the *Adadya.*

Passent cannot attend high school because she

cannot leave the Islahaya to attend a normal school and

there is no money available for this to happen. She has

nowhere to live, no one to take her in while attending

high school. Her dreams of becoming a doctor at the

moment are just that, dreams. All the years Hanna has

been working with Agouza, only three girls have

completed their *Thanawa,* and they had families who

allowed them to come home as long as they attended school. Passent has no one and certainly no one to whom she can turn for any education beyond high school if she ever did manage the exams. Family life betrayed Passent, society brushes her aside.

****

Selection of a marriage partner engages most members of the family; in particular the women, mothers, sisters, and female cousins search for a prospective groom for their daughter, and in some cases, a man's family will also search out a suitable woman for their son. Discussion of partners involves another family conclave which gathers to discuss the merits of possible mates. Many Egyptian families still prefer to keep marriages within the extended family. First cousins often marry; if no first cousins are available, then second or third cousins may suit. A shopping list of mates is drawn up creating charts comparing the various candidates; then weeks of dispute ensue until a final list is decided upon. The decision for a marriage partner does not really rest with the prospective bride or groom, but with the family.

If a female wants to go out of the home to work, although the law says she may, the man's family sees this as a strong veto for marriage. A woman should be content to stay at home, have many children, especially sons, and if she must work to supplement family income, let it be for only a few hours a day usually cooking or cleaning for a wealthy family. Does she wish for a social life? If so, this, too, is a negative. Social life and activities are reserved for sons, husbands, brothers, fathers, in other words, male family members. Their activities outside the home cannot be questioned. A wife needs to be content indoors with children and other women, whether neighbours or family. To be seen going out with friends, desiring a social life is for the husband to decide. Again, though the law says a woman has this right, family tradition and culture are so deep that substitutes for actual law.

Education is only attainable for girls of the upper or wealthy classes. According to tradition and custom, the attitude is that females do not require much education; they will be home taking care of children. Too many below-legal-age marriages take place in the rural country areas. Often families in a desire to get rid of their daughters will lie about a girl's age. Many marry as young as ten or twelve providing a man can be found. Frequently, many older men, perhaps looking for a third or fourth wife, will take a young girl as his wife. Many poor families willingly give their daughters if the price is right. Several Islahaya girls have had this unfortunate experience of being sold in marriage. It is a form of sex-trafficking, and many of these girls run away from families and husbands.

With so much poverty in Egypt and the cost of marriage so very high, those from other cultures might ask why a push for marriage and early marriage. There are several reasons for this. One, in the Muslim world pre-marital sex is *haram*, and although prostitution is practiced and prostitutes readily available, it is illegal and the punishments for being a prostitute are severe often including death. Any man caught with a prostitute could be jailed. Second, having children is an integral part of Muslim society. Third, even though *haram* and punishable by death or imprisonment, homosexuality exists. Marriage, even one of convenience, allays any suspicions about a son's sexuality.

It isn't the law which need to change for the Islahaya girls. It is the attitude, government responsibility, and education which will give these girls a new, clean life. It's the government which needs to clear the girls' records and erase the stigma of police file from their names. Egypt and Egyptians owe them the same fresh start in the name of law, society, and the hope which is driving its people towards its own new beginnings.

Chapter Six

Egypt Then and Now

Driving through Cairo in the American University of Cairo car the first day of my arrival, absorbing sights and sounds, taking in all the city had to offer, I never felt any of the homesickness often accompanying decisions to leave one's homeland. In a city of twenty million, Cairo teems with activity, crowded streets, and throngs of people, cars, busses, and noise day and night.

Cairo traffic

Mr Ashraf, the AUC representative, collected me at the airport and in spite of seemingly endless hours of travel, sleep eluded me as he showed me monuments, statues, landmarks as we navigated the maze of traffic.

We stopped at his very ancient Coptic Church along the way, a place he explained that had its foundation in the escape to Egypt by the Holy Family. Legend has it the family hid from the Roman soldiers in the darkened recesses inside the Church walls. As I stepped onto the broken curbing into the faded light inside the Church, a smell soon to be familiar odour assailed my senses, a combination of food, smog, dirt, diesel, sweaty bodies, and sweet smelling perfumes, flowers, created a uniquely Egyptian essence. Sometimes overpowering, often distasteful, occasionally pleasant, Egypt boasts its own special aura.

Typical street scene in Cairo, vendor selling on back of donkey cart

Interspersed with the everyday sights, sounds, and smells of Egypt; the magnificence of its historical past looms on virtually every corner. Not merely the monuments transported from their original sites now sitting majestically along some of Cairo's more luxurious boulevards and parks, but the sensation of ancient wisdom, civilization, culture, and heritage emanate from the atmosphere of Cairo and by extension the country, Egypt.

What then is Egypt? Geographically situated in the Middle East, the Mediterranean Sea its northern border; Egypt extends east into the Sinai Peninsula with the Red Sea marking its eastern border as it divides the Western Sinai with the northern Red Sea which eventually flows into the Mediterranean via the Suez Canal. Part of the Red Sea becomes the Gulf of Aqaba which borders Saudi Arabia on the east and Jordan to the north.

To the south Egypt shares its border with Sudan with her westernmost neighbour is Libya. The magical Nile, the world's longest river, flows from the south.

A beautiful sunset on the Nile

It's the river pouring life's blood into those who rely on its water; it's the river of history, civilization, heritage, the river upon which so much depends. Because of its northerly flow, its main source coming from Lake Victoria. Southern Egypt is still referred to as Upper Egypt and the area beginning around Helwan just south of Cairo and through Alexandria to the Mediterranean is considered Lower Egypt.

Egypt and her people embody an ancient civilization with its cultural heritage, from a series of conquests of Egypt dating from Alexander the Great in 330 BCE through the twentieth century under British Colonial rule. It wasn't until the early 1950s Egypt's secular, revolutionary leadership under Abdel Gamal Nasser (1956-1970, Egypt's second president after the overthrow of King Farouk) that Egypt began its ascent into modern politics. After the success of this political coup major changes began which have led to the events of Egypt's Arab Spring of 25 January 2011 and the second sudden change of events of 30 June 2013.

Tourists flock to exhibits of Tutankhamen's burial mask and the many other golden and wonderful artefacts discovered in his tomb when uncovered in 1922. The glories of Abu Simbel south of Aswan, the magnificence of Karnak temple in Luxor, or the Valley of the Kings, Queens, and workers residing on Luxor's west bank draw millions of tourists every year who

view in awe the final resting places where their lives are

told in the beautiful painted hieroglyphs lining the

tombs.[23]

Temple columns from Abu Simbel

---

[23]A note on Egypt's tourism since the election of Morsi and the rise of the Muslim Brotherhood to power: tourism is failing and the lack of revenue into the country is leading to an increase in gangs and crime. Prices are rising, fuel, food, and most necessities are in scarce supply, theft is on the rise, and conditions are not improving. Morsi's political security is being threatened by continual demonstrations. The outcome of all these problems is at best a daily guessing game.

Paintings inside tombs – Valley of the Kings -Luxor

Egypt's Sphinx protecting the Great Pyramid

Egypt's major cities sit near or on the Nile's banks as most of the country is desert; cultivation is difficult without the Nile waters. In the 1950s, President Nasser had the Aswan Dam built in the city of Aswan, very near the Sudanese border, although with many benefits, it also has been the object of much environmental controversy.

In Cairo, Medan Tahrir (Tahrir Square) symbolizes change in much the same fashion as the monuments to Ramses II symbolize an Egypt of magnificent glory. Tahrir is surrounded by shops, the Egyptian Museum, the *Mogama* or government building, and the American University in Cairo.[24]

To understand their need for a new future, it's relevant to look at Egypt's recent past. What created

---

[24] Although the American University (AUC) has relocated to New Cairo, a new suburb in the eastern desert outside Cairo, the American University still maintains a few of its buildings adjacent to Tahrir Square.

that volcanic action in January 2011 that finally burst

the patience of a people who by nature are kind and

whose favourite phrase is *mafish mushkila*.[25] The

country, rich from its cotton exports, heavy tourism,

fruit, vegetables, and other commodities, gave Nasser

the opportunity to establish what in his own mind,

would create a better Egypt. He did begin a series of

industrial development, factories, mass production of

various goods and products. He also opened a new era

of culture in Egypt. Radio, television, theatre, literary

societies flourished under Nasser's regime. However,

he established a strict political rule, elections were only

superficial and he began a purge of some of his closest

lieutenants, those immediately involved in the original

political coup deposing the king. Any criticism saw

many of these men disappearing from public life. Some

---

[25] *Mafish mushkila* means no worries, no problem.

were made house prisoners, others left Egypt in exile, and others merely vanished.

Nasser began to open the Egyptian coffers to politicians and journalists and others in order to gain support for his many enterprises. These included unnecessary involvement in wars in the African Congo, Katanga, and Yemen for example. Nasser shipped water to Saudi Arabia along with money to Lebanon, Syria, and Iraq. The Egyptian pound, at the beginning of Nasser's rule, equalled the value of one British guinea, in 1956 a substantial amount of money. Nasser's ultimate desire was to be an acknowledged Middle Eastern force. He made alliances with countries not necessarily amenable to the Western powers, i.e. the Soviet Union, to help him with major projects like the Aswan Dam.

Nasser was a socialist; he revamped his society in socialist philosophy, spent money without thinking of the consequences which by the early 1960s rose to phenomenal heights, making it necessary for him to create a new currency, and inflate the Egyptian pound. This inflation created havoc for many of the established Egyptians, the money they had in banks lost value, some lost everything in many transactions. He also filled his treasury by taking land from plantation owners and subdividing this land into smaller units, giving to each farmer five fidams (about five acres). While currying favour with the small landholder, this tactic reduced Egypt's agricultural output for overseas trade. Inheritance practices too came into the picture. These are guided by *Shari'a* law meaning that among sons, the division of land was equal. The land suffered so many divisions and subdivisions that export farming could no longer be sustained, all that was left was very tiny

subsistence farms on which poor farmers subsisted.[26]

In 1967 with the advent and loss of the Five-Day

War against the Israelis, Egyptian pride sank to its

lowest ebb. Convinced by Nasser they were invincible,

young Egyptians flocked to this cause, only to be

decimated in five short days. In one swoop, for the

second time in eleven years, Egypt lost its pride of place,

the Sinai became Israeli territory. Not until after

Nasser's death did the Egyptians invade the Sinai, push

the Israeli army back to regain most of the Sinai. In

1979 under President Anwar Sadat of Egypt (1970-

1981) and President Carter of the USA and the

controversial Camp David Accords did Egypt regain the

last small piece of the Sinai, Taba Heights. Visitors to

---

[26] This form of dividing land was practiced during the early Middle Ages in Europe, called *gavelkind,* eventually found to be ineffective for the very same reasons, too much subdividing and land becomes worthless, its only value is subsistence living.

Taba now come to a lovely hotel, very blue and clear

Red Sea waters, and just at the entrance to the Sinai a

gate locking Palestinians out of Egypt.

Resort and the twelfth century crusader fort built by Sala al Din

(Saladin) – adjacent to the Egypt/Palestine border – Taba

Over hundreds of years, through changes in

dynasty and rulers, Egyptians had been slowly stripped

of the knowledge and will to self-govern successfully.

Nasser and then Sadat continued this process. But Sadat opened Egypt up to trade, industry, capitalist ventures from any and all who wished to participate, which gained him a better reputation in the West. However, shortly prior to his assassination in 1981, Sadat began arresting any who criticised the government, Sadat and his policies. These men and women were put in prison for indeterminate lengths of time.

One person deserves mention especially as her fight for women's issues and rights strikes at the heart of this book. Her name is Nawal el Sadaawi. She suffered at the hands of Anwar Sadat and was imprisoned for her outspoken attacks on the government and its policies toward women. She has spent a lifetime attempting to make changes in the lives of Egyptian women, including making public the terrible practice of FGM. For her efforts, her written work, protest campaigns, Nawal has known much ridicule and persecution, yet her voice has been heard and voices like hers are needed to make changes in the lives of Egypt's young girls. Imprisoned in 1981 under Sadat, Nawal was released one month after his assassination; however, it wasn't until the early twenty-first century that her writings were not banned in Egypt. She afterwards wrote about her time in prison 'Danger has been a part of my life ever since I picked up a pen and wrote. Nothing is more perilous than truth in a world that lies'.

Egypt developed a secular constitution, a continuation of past colonial rule, not one based on *Shari'a* law.[27] Egypt's unique population demographics make it difficult to impose strict *Shari'a* law; roughly

---

[27] *Shari'a* law is law based on the Qur'an and would create an Islamic state such as Saudi Arabia or any of the other Gulf States, while secular law is civil law as countries in the West practice, i.e., Great Britain, France, Germany, or America. However, Egypt does incorporate *Shari'a* law for divorce and family issues, making it a very complex set of rules and regulations to follow. For some things secular laws are used, for others, religious laws apply.

ten-fifteen percent are Coptic, Orthodox or Western

Christians. Egypt's constitution declares that although

Islam is the state religion, all religions must be treated

fairly and equally.[28] In essence, the constitution was

civil, based on the French model or the Napoleonic

Code; but other legal aspects, such as marriage and

inheritance for Muslims have a *Shari'a* foundation.

After Sadat's assassination in 1981 by a radical

Islamist Egyptian, Hosni Mubarak (1981-2011) took

over the reins of government. For the first years, he

continued most of Sadat's policies, but allowed open

criticism of government, politics, and other aspects of

society. As a relative unknown in political circles,

Mubarak paved his way with care. Not until midway

---

[28] However, with the Muslim Brotherhood and Morsi and their new constitution, these old provisions are eroding slowly but with the interim government now in power, it has declared a reinstitution of the old constitution until such time as an elected government can write a new constitution.

through his thirty year reign did things noticeably unravel for the Egyptian people.

The Mubarak regime eventually became equated with corruption. Mubarak established trusted lieutenants in key positions, seeking to establish what has become an incredible maze of government cover-ups, siphoning of funds, at the expense of the Egyptian people. Money came pouring into the coffers of the Egyptian treasury from the West, money meant for programmes for Egypt, which never seemed to make it to its designated destinations.

Where did the foreign billions go? The money never saw its way to the poorest sectors of Egypt. Children went hungry, schools failed to get needed resources, parents never ceased in their daily struggle to feed large families, and the jobless numbers grew. Alongside these poor Egyptians, the rich drive in their luxury cars, travel the world, spend money on the best clothes, live in sumptuous flats, and receive excellent educations. At the bottom, the poorest of all, the children of the street roam during the day and at night search for a place to sleep, a crust of bread to eat, and sometimes for families who deserted them. These children, girls and boys, live among the rich, the struggling poor, the waning middle class, and the tourists who come to visit relics of Egypt's past splendour.

Egyptian museum - a backdrop for construction and revolutionary demonstrations in Medan Tahrir

Egypt then, before the revolution, was tangled in so many directions. The streets jammed with automobiles, the rich intermingled with the poor, who multiply faster than the economy can adjust to their needs. Education mocks itself in its inefficiencies at all levels. Elementary, middle, and higher education, unless private institutions, lack qualified teachers, willing pupils, encouraging parents, parents with funds enough to educate their children. Result ? A society with minimal functional literacy, especially among women, confusion and chaos among Egypt's poorest struggling to survive.

Rich and poor, Muslim and Christian, tourist and resident, foreigner and Egyptian cross the ultra busy streets of Cairo and its other cities.

Typical Egyptian street scene

Donkey carts join busy auto traffic, bread men balance flats of *baladi* bread[29] on their heads as they ride bicycles through the thronging traffic. Street stall owners sell their wares from carts adjoining shops which have survived in some form through many generations.

---

[29] Baladi bread is the typical Egyptian flat bread similar to what in the West is termed pita bread.

Tariq, a local shop owner, proudly displays picture of his grandfather who started the business in the 1930s

Street seller among shops and traffic

Cars, taxis by the thousands, motor bikes with families balancing three or four children; wife on the back, nestling an infant in her arms weave through heavy congestion or in Arabic *zakhma* (noise, confusion). Rubbish, discarded cigarettes, unsightly faeces from the plethora of stray cats and dogs litter the streets. Bleeping of horns, loud voices, children screeching in playgrounds all add to the cacophonic Cairene atmosphere. Cairo's odour, a stench arising from humanity, animals, cars, smog, and dirt, desert dust, combined with the twice annual *mousin* enveloping the city adds its thick blanket of blackness to the atmosphere.[30] In spite of this amalgamation of humanity, Cairo's citizens are gentle, mostly kind, up till now, patient. This was Cairo then.

---

[30] *Mousin* is a fierce wind and dust storm that emanates from the desert and attacks the city with gusto, covering everything with dust, the remnants of animal droppings, and anything else that flies in its fierce wind.

Then Cairo and all Egypt erupted. Most street
scenes remained the same, but with an indisputable
difference. Reporters, cameras, international television
media converged on the city covering the stunning
events, the Arab Spring revolution of 25 January 2011
demanding the resignation of President Hosni Mubarak.

*Waiting patiently in Tahrir Square for announcement of Mubarak's
resignation*

Initially the Mubarak regime attempted to
silence these reporters, fearing the consequences of
global reaction to the events in Tahrir. Phone lines for

outside the country were cut, internet access denied to

the general populace. Their efforts were unsuccessful;

the world heard the stunning news that the people of

Egypt demanded their leader step down. The people

demanded democracy, freedom of speech and change in

the way their leaders ran the country. Get rid of

corruption, give us the vote, work, and lower prices for

food so we can all eat! These became the revolutionary

slogans, as was the cry to keep America out of their bid

for democracy, "It's our problem, America, not yours!"

Demonstrators of 25 January 2011 revolution in Tahrir Square

Tahrir Square buzzed with activity, anyone could enter with a passport or identity card, the queues extended around the length of the corniche[31] for over a mile. I watched these events on television in the safety of my home across the Persian Gulf in the Emirates. Booked to leave for Egypt on the 25th of January, those plans suddenly changed, flights into Egypt were cancelled, but watching was not good enough. I finally reached my friends in Cairo by phone, and realized I needed to be there with them, see and hear for myself the unfolding events which I did. I took the next flight out and joined the crowds in Medan Tahrir.

Surprisingly, the mood inside Tahrir was peaceful. Rising to an unspoken challenge, those entering the square massed together in an invisible bond, a bond essential for achieving freedom. The

---

[31] *Corniche* is used in the Arab expression for any promenade or front along the seaside or as in the case of Cairo, the Nile River.

square teemed with goodwill, camaraderie, and time

closed in on the demand, "Step down Mubarak!"

Waiting for good news, the resignation of Mubarak – January 2011

Excitement built and when Mubarak finally

announced his resignation, the air exploded with

uncontrollable joy, dancing in the square, on the streets,

and in the neighbourhoods. Hope reigned. It took

Egyptians days to come down from this euphoria. As

exaltation subsided into some semblance of normality,

the city itself began to take on a different hue. Streets

were cleaned, rubbish removed from the curbs, animal droppings swept away, walkways painted for the first time in decades, store fronts glistened with polish. For Egypt change seemed imminent, inevitable.

Egyptians became despondent. Cairo's streets reverted to their old look, rubbish began piling up once again, and shopkeepers despaired as tourism, one of Egypt's richest commodities, declined to a virtual standstill. The economy worsened, resorts suffered losses and continue to do so. The question looms, where is democracy? What argument could be made for this "freedom," after all what good does it do to be able to criticize a government, its leaders, its policies, if bread cannot be put on the table? Tensions mounted, friendly faces disappeared in brows furrowed in worry as conditions worsened, prices increased, while work decreased. No exports, no imports, no tourists, no income, little food.

Sadly, as the weeks dragged on, then months, change did not take place. For the first year, the military reneged on its promise to step down after six months. Tensions among the politicians rose, political parties collided, revolutionary figures evaporated in the midst of confusion. Who or what would emerge as the "new Egypt"? Amidst this, the Muslim Brotherhood rose to command leadership in spite of their promise to stay in the background. No single individual emerged to run for presidential office, scrapping began in the papers, on the news while international coverage decreased. Elections for a new government stalled. Finally in September 2012 elections were held. Were these elections fully democratic? They had the semblance of fairness and democracy, but who actually voted and how did they know for whom to vote? Illiterate voters could only elect a picture, issues were not clearly defined, the Muslim Brotherhood, with its reputation of supporting the very poor, took advantage of its position.

Unfortunately, the revolutionary architects, engaged in

in-fighting, did not develop a cohesive unit, one that

could defeat a party whose ultimate goal was to create

an Islamic state, not a democratic state.

So as of June 2013, dissidents again rose up in protest.

Souhail Hosni and Hanna Hartmann-Hosni in Tahrir Square

30 June 2013 cheering for change

They wanted a clearly defined secular state, not a religious one under Shari'a law. The world still awaits the outcome of what is becoming a country increasingly violent and lawless. Factions are divided, those who support deposed president Morsi and the Muslim Brotherhood, and those fighting for a secular state, one that fulfils its promises of creating jobs, making food available to all, and bringing a renewal of the now failing tourist trade. Sadly, Mohammed el Baradei, a voice for diplomacy and reason, resigned from the interim government formed in early July 2013. He gave his rationale as discouragement over the violence and inability of the interim government and the military to contain and change this situation.

Rubbish piling up on city streets once again-disillusion setting in

So far nothing is settled. The world watches daily news reports, we hear about violence in the streets, we see what the reporters want to show us. But in reality cars continue to jam the streets; smog, pollution, and noise disturb the air as always, people struggle for a few piasters, for any chance to scratch a living. Every Friday, the holy day in Islam, after noon prayers, Tahrir Square once again fills with rally cries in efforts to improve their living conditions. The outcry for democracy can be heard from most Egyptians, while on another side of the city demonstrations in support of the deposed president Morsi continue.

Through all this turmoil one element of Egyptian society remained and remains neglected. *Il Binait Dol,* those girls living in the Islahaya, those children roaming Cairo's streets, those young, ignored but a growing part of Egypt's population, has no one to look after them, to care for them. They have no voice, who will even listen? Their buildings remain in disrepair; their lives become more desolate than ever.

Living conditions inside the Islahaya – dirt and grime everywhere

Through all these strikes, demonstrations, and rallies, nothing is done for the street girls, the girls neglected by everyone. With Egypt's political and economic situation as it stands now it will take more energy to bring this sad and interminable state of affairs for street girls to an end. But it is time to give them a

voice, let them be heard, give them a chance to be.

Chapter Seven

Will it Ever Change?

To the uninitiated or those who have never visited the Middle East, understanding the multi-layered tiers of life among Middle Eastern people is extremely complex. Unfortunately, since the tragedy of 9/11, many non-Middle Easterners, in particular non-Muslims, find it difficult to get past the word terrorist when discussing this part of the world. It takes months, even years, of living in any of these countries to obtain insight into this complex society. When I first moved to Cairo, my initial impressions were noise, heat, dirt, dust, and history, not necessarily in that order, but the implosion to the senses hits even before leaving the airport.

The first multi-ethnic, multi-cultural images of Cairo emerged with a 'bang' as we picked our way slowly through throngs of cars obliterated much of the real Cairo, the real Egypt. The country's mysteries, its past, its magic obscures the impoverished, suffering reality which lay barely beneath the surface. It took time, understanding, and hours with Egyptian students and friends to comprehend this very ancient culture.

Market day in a northern Egyptian town of Rasheed

258

Minarets towering above the Cairo skyline

To the Westerner immersed in knowledge of basic legal and human rights, constitutional guarantees, freedom of choice, speech, movement, and everything else to which we are accustomed, the intricacies of a society in which the roots are tradition, family, religion, and *"insha' Allah"*[32] boggles the mind. Even this simple phrase

---

[32] *Insha'Allah* loosely means as Allah wills. It is said with virtually every statement, particularly when the statement has to do with attending something, going somewhere. My students stretched it to mean they may or may not turn in assignments or even come to

insha Allah, which to any Middle Easterner is part of every conversation, loosely meaning if Allah wills, then whatever is planned will happen according to Allah's will, often has Westerners thinking this is merely an excuse for non-compliance or at worst failure.

****

Alia's story – told in 2007:

When I was four years old my mother locked the door on me and would not allow me back in. I just wandered the streets of our small village. I remember crying and wandering around, banging on the door to our house, but my mother wouldn't let me in. I don't know the name of the town, or how I got here to Cairo. I did creep onto a cart to sleep one night and the next day it left the town. I just stayed on it until the man driving it found me. He let me stay, but I was scared and left him. I walked and

---

class. For those of us not used to qualifying every statement we make, this is a difficult and often obstructive idea to master.

walked, finally I guess I came to Cairo but soon the police picked me up and brought me here. I don't know anything else, except that I have to be here, I have no name, no family, and nothing. Madam Ibtisam lets me take these classes and I hope to learn how to read and write. There is nothing else.

Have you ever been beaten or punished here?

No, I just do what they tell me so it's okay. It's the only home I have, and I don't want to go on the streets again.

Alia is still resident at this Islahaya in 2013.

Alia, 2011

****

Zeinab's story – told to Nevien in 2011:

Zeinab, can you tell me how you came to the Islahaya?

I was thrown out of the home when I was seven. But I didn't come here right away. I lived on the streets for a long time. A gang picked me up soon after I left the home and forced me to sell fruit or tissues on the streets. They made me give them all the money I earned and if I didn't they wouldn't feed me. Sometimes I had to go out on the streets late at night just to find a piece of bread or food thrown out in the garbage. I was very dirty all the time, and people pushed me away, most of the time I didn't even have shoes. The gang thought it was better; maybe people would feel sorry for me. I was very young.

What else happened to you when you were on the streets? What else did the gang members do to you?

The older boys and some of the girls raped me because I was too young to fight them off.

How long did you stay with the gang?

I'm not sure but at least three years. You see, I had nowhere else to go and I was getting to be a very good beggar child. I learned all the tricks, people, especially the tourists, felt sorry for me and would give me money. When they did, I found a place to hide some of it and not give it to the gang. They still don't know about the secret money I have and one day when I leave here I will get it and have some money.

You're not afraid that someone found it and has stolen your money?

No, it's very safe!

Did anything else happen to you on the outside?

When I was about eleven, I think, I earned money sleeping with older men. I found a place under the bridge (Kasr el Nil) and they would come and ask for me. I think they liked me because I was still very young. They paid me, not much, but I added this money to my hiding place.

What happened to bring you to the Islahaya?

One night, under the bridge, two policemen came and pushed me into their car. They raped me first, then brought me to their station where they put me in a back room. They raped me again and then they finally brought me here to this Islahaya.

Did you know how to read or write before you came here?

No I couldn't read or write at all, but after a while the supervisors have been letting me take classes with Madam Hala. I really want to learn, and right now I know my alphabet in Arabic, but it's really hard for me. Sometimes I just give up and act tough, like some of the girls who don't take classes.

Where will you go when you leave here? When will you leave?

Madam Hala (one of the Directors) says that I have to leave in about three or four years. But I don't know where I'll go or what to do? There's no one out there for me, I have no family and I don't have too many friends inside. What can I do? I have to leave.

Zeinab at seventeen

****

Noussa's dreams as told to Nevien in 2012:

I lived in an orphanage until I was ten and then they sent me away to this Islahaya. I've been here since then and I am now nineteen years old. The Directors told me that I have to leave in two years, but where can I go? I have no papers, no family and since I came from the orphanage, no identity of any kind. Madam Hanna is trying to help so that I can take the Adadaya and maybe go to high school. That's what I want more than anything but I don't know if it can happen.

If you can't get papers or finish school, do you know what you will do? Where will you go? (At this point Noussa was in tears, she could barely answer Nevien's questions.)

I don't know, I just don't know. Can anyone help me?

Noussa at nineteen

****

What do Noussa or any of the other girls need for their dreams to come true? Their needs are fairly simple and basic. A place to live and money on which to live while studying, but the government neither provides these nor at this point is it willing to entertain the idea for girls. Education provides the best way out of a life of misery and deprivation for *Il Binait Dol* rather than a marriage that may or may not work. Yet, the authorities have not been bothered with the welfare of its female street girls. Hanna has written to the Minister of Social Affairs, Dr Gouda Abdel Khalid, regarding the general welfare and needs of the girls, their substandard housing and overall lack of interest displayed toward these girls, but neither he nor his board of directors seem to care. The board's head, a Mr Abdulla, is well past his prime, deaf, and rather insensitive to their needs, and works with his associate Mr Mounir. Each governorate has its own board for their Islahayas; in the

Giza governorate Madame Hala replaced Mahmoud al

Fakahani as head of the Giza Social Affairs Directorate,

but still shows no interest in improving the situation in

the Islahayas for girls.

Hanna first appealed to the new director,

Madame Hala, regarding the girls' excursion to Ras

Sudr. Claiming ignorance, Madame Hala promised to

investigate the situation, but either she felt powerless in

her new position to make strenuous recommendations,

or she had no desire to interfere with the ongoing

decision to deny the trip. In the end, neither Hanna's

appeals nor her husband's to the Ministry of Social

Affairs and then to the Ministry of Education reaped any

results; the girls were denied their summer outing and

the money raised by Hanna and her Social Committee

went elsewhere.

A sum of £1,000,000 Egyptian per Islahaya (142,857US) is banked each year to be used towards the girls' annual upkeep just in the Agouza Islahaya. Hanna estimates about £30,000 Egyptian (4,286US) per month is needed to feed all the girls and the staff, around 120 people with three meals per day. Even if this figure is accurate, £640,000 Egyptian (91,429US) remains. Where does it go? Certainly not for supplies, mattresses, hygiene, clothes, or small excursions out of the Islahaya; these treats all come from the efforts of Hanna and her Social Committee. If the money is not used, it is not carried over for the next year's budget. The Ministry puts it back into some other general fund or somewhere that cannot be identified. With numerous Islahayas in the Cairo area and none with Hanna as their protector and provider, how much unused money from the £1,000,000 Egyptian remains to go into unknown pockets? If the Agouza Islahaya is indicative of the lack of care given to the *Il Benait Dol*, then serious questions need answering. Surely money can be found to provide proper education and better living standards for the girls as it is for the boys.

There is a plethora of stories similar to that of Zeinab, Mona, Noussa and the other girls. The result is still the same, where can they go, what can they do, and will these conditions ever change? One incident which happened to a student of mine when she was going to the Islahaya in 2006 best illustrates the frustration felt by everyone working to improve the condition of the Islahaya girls, *Il Binait Dol.*

****

Alia and Ayesha – 2007:

One of my more ambitious students, Alia, spent more than the required ten hours at the Islahaya. Her humanitarian spirit stirred at the girls' plight; she felt

the need to encourage the girls to confide in her, she

brought small articles of clothing for them to share

around, some books for the girls in school, and

generally established a very good relationship with

these girls. Unfortunately, she ignored one instruction–

-under no circumstances give out your personal

information, i.e., address, phone number, email address,

or anything else which might enable the girls to get in

contact.

One of the girls, Ayesha, became Alia's special

project. Ayesha's life was especially tragic, scars

marked her arms from self-mutilation, she had been

raped before age ten by an uncle, beaten repeatedly by a

step-mother, and worst of all, in her mind, either

completely ignored or beaten with brutal force by her

father. Unable to withstand the pain, emotional and

physical, Ayesha, aged eleven, ran away from her home

in a small village in Upper Egypt. How she made her

way north to Cairo remains a mystery. Ayesha came to

the huge city frightened and most definitely alone.

Accosted by a street gang of both girls and boys,

Ayesha fell in with this crowd. Needless to say, her life

with them became a continuation of life in her home.

Forced into prostitution, forced to either steal or sell the

unending supply of tissues, lemons, and mint prevalent

on Cairo's streets, Ayesha soon found herself in another

hell. She is not sure how long she lived and worked

with this street gang, but Ayesha eventually came into

police custody and was then brought to Agouza. Within

weeks, she knew her fate was tied intrinsically with this

Islahaya, so she quickly learned the ropes, played the

game to gain the director's permission for extra

privileges. Madam Ibtisam, the then director of Agouza,

soon gave Ayesha the right to attend the small classes

with Hanna's teachers, and this is how she became acquainted with my students.

One day during the semester, I received a frantic phone call from Alia; Ayesha had run away from the Islahaya, something she had often done during the night only to return during the day. She used sexual favours with the guard to escape; Ayesha is not the only girl to use this tactic. Ayesha's life outside included more than prostitution and selling for the gang, they got her hooked on drugs. She became addicted; therefore, found ways to escape from Agouza at night, regardless of the risks, to meet up with the gang. Each time they would give her drugs, but demanded sex in return. For her, as with so many of the girls, sex to them meant warmth and comfort, a form of love, human connection. For Ayesha, at eleven, the cycle had begun. By age twelve when she entered Agouza, she was street-wise, sly, and smart. She knew how to play all the systems to get what she wanted. When she met my students, however, another year had passed; she was thirteen, or at least that's the age she believed, and through Hanna's generosity, and the teachers' patience, we hoped Ayesha's behaviour would change.

Alia believed that a girl like Ayesha, so abused all her life, really desired to turn her life around. But escaping from the Islahaya was exactly wrong. Alia had given her phone number to Ayesha, and with a stolen mobile phone, in the middle of the night Ayesha called Alia for help. Alia's parents, very kind and forward-thinking themselves, agreed to let the girl come to them that night; they gave her a hot meal, a warm bed in which to sleep, helped her clean herself up, and provided fresh clothes. That night is when Alia phoned me and the chain of phone calls began as Ayesha's escape and subsequent complications set in. Alia, her parents, AUC, the police, Hanna and her Social

Committee, and of course, the Islahaya, all had to be involved in figuring a solution for this one run-away.

I phoned my department chair and also the Dean; they both agreed Alia and her parents needed to be guided by the police, as Ayesha's primary custodial issues came from them. Alia's mother, Noor, a businesswoman in her own right, wanted to help Ayesha. She offered to take the girl in, train her in domestic skills, cooking, cleaning, and also to see that she continued her education. However, she consulted an attorney who went with her to the local police. The police official laughed, called her a fool to attempt any rehabilitation with a girl like Ayesha, and told her 'she's a criminal now and always will be. You'll wake up one morning to find all your valuables stolen, maybe one of your children harmed, someone killed.'

This police official refused to sign the waiver to release Ayesha from the Islahaya. Noor and her attorney went higher, but came up against the same mocking attitude and refusal to sign the release. The authorities frightened Noor sufficiently that she eventually withdrew her support. With two younger children in the house, Noor believed the police; Ayesha could never change, did not want to change, and although very sorry for Ayesha, Noor had to choose between her own family and assisting one girl out of a life of degradation and poverty. Neither Hanna nor her Social Committee had enough influence with the police or the Minister of Social Affairs to obtain Ayesha's release. Hanna wrote several times to the then First Lady Suzanne Mubarak beseeching her assistance, not only for Ayesha, but for the deplorable conditions in which the girls lived. But after two or three letters with no reply from Mrs Mubarak's office, they could do no more.

What happened to Ayesha? For her infractions, she has been shipped off to an Islahaya far from Cairo which practices very strict incarceration for its girls, removed from any possibility of further education, and virtually cut off from outside contact. Hanna attempted some investigation, but the Ministry stopped her. No contact with another Islahaya would be allowed. An inhumane ending for a girl who reached out for kindness, help, and in her short life began to realize the importance of education. Ayesha's story does not stand alone; there are hundreds like her. Hanna, Noor, Alia, and everyone connected with this event, realize the extent of work which needs to be done to make positive changes.

****

Possibilities

The Revolutions of 2011 and 2013 have had a debilitating affect on the Islahayas and their inmates. The law has not been kind, in fact it has been harsher towards women. Although the Ministries changed from Mubarak to the military and then the Muslim Brotherhood and once again in a state of flux with the interim government and all the problems assailing Egypt as of August 2013, ministers fail to consider the plight of these girls. The Muslim Brotherhood with Mohammed Morsi as president demonstrated their attitude in general towards women and as a by-product of this attitude it's no wonder that physical conditions in the Islahaya degenerated.[33] If Agouza is indicative of the hundreds of Islahayas around the country, then Egypt's shame grows incrementally, rather than decreasing with the supposed upward and positive

[33] See above discussion for changes in the political system.

changes which were the original intentions of the 2013 Revolution.

The newest Minister of Social Affairs must take positive action; appoint local overseers who will take the lead in righting the conditions in which the girls live.

****

Contrast

While living in the UAE, I became acquainted with a woman in Dubai, the aunt of one of my students. Nadia trained as a social worker and practiced in this field for twenty-five years although she came from a very wealthy and influential family. Nadia is different from many post -1971 Emiratis (the year the Emirates became a country). She works diligently, her concern for the homeless and helpless children in the UAE drive her ambitions.[34] After a successful career as social worker in the Dubai Emirate, Nadia decided to open a home for the severely handicapped and homeless street children. Initially, she rented a house for the children, brought in teachers at her own expense, assigned one-to-one care givers for the handicapped children, and provided money for the street children to attend school. In 2010, her efforts and project came to the attention of Sheikh Mohammed bin Rashid al Maktoum, the ruling Sheikh of Dubai and vice president of the Emirates. He generously donated land, right across from the prestigious Jumeira Beach, built her a residential school for her street children, boys and girls, which also included facilities for her day care handicapped children.

---

[34] With the change to the Emirates because of the oil and oil wealth, many Emirates do not feel any financial stress or the need to work, therefore Nadia, coming from one of the wealthiest Emirati families, chose to pour her energies, talents, and money into improving and helping the disabled and displaced homeless children of the Emirates.

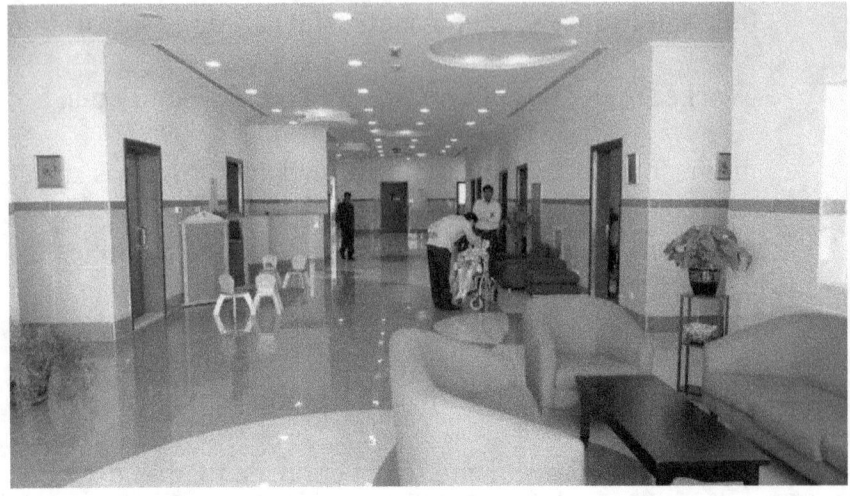

Entry way to Senses – the Dubai Islahaya run by Madam Nadia

The Sheikh now provides water and electricity for the facilities, but the rest of the operating money comes from donations and Nadia's extensive fund-raising efforts. Nadia employs staff to care for the handicapped children, teachers to instruct those able to learn, provides a physician who sees to the children's needs, who lives in the facilities during the week. She also has cooks, four in total, three men and one woman, who make simple but very nourishing meals for her children.

Cooking in pristine facilities

The severely handicapped children come from families who cannot afford expensive care so she takes these children in on a day-to-day basis.

All children are cared for equally, boys and girls

I met one little girl, a street orphan, left and neglected on Dubai's streets with half her face bitten off by stray dogs. Nadia took her in. She is just learning to speak; when she first came to the Dubai Islahaya, she could not speak or smile.

With care and medical help she may one day talk and walk

Today, with the aid of her nurses and continuous physical therapy, this is changing for her, as are her facial injuries which have begun to repair and heal with proper medical care.

The facilities are pristine; those children who are Dubai's street children have bedrooms decked out in pink for the girls and blue for the boys, each with a small kitchen (no stoves) but a small refrigerator and sink.

Pink for girls, blue for boys

Here they learn the basics of self-caring. All the children have chores; they must keep their own space tidy. Nadia insists they learn these skills as they are life skills everyone needs to have.

This is one small example of what is being done in the Emirates under the patronage of the Sheikh and Emirati law. Nadia showed me the identity cards, medical cards, and papers which each child possesses.

Emirati law declares that these children must have provisions such as this, including her street children who have no homes or families other than

Nadia, whom they call "mom." These children, unlike Egyptian street children, have protection under the law and are entitled to citizenship, even though parentage is unknown. They are entitled to education, passports, complete identity, and a place within Emirati society. As for their education, most of the street children who have come to Nadia are too old and also illiterate for regular public schooling, so Nadia must find and fund their private schools, which she does. In total, she has 120 children, fifty of whom are street children with no families. The others are the severely handicapped who go home to their families in the evening.

When I asked the difficult question, how many street children are there in the Emirates, or just Dubai, she did hesitate a bit. Emirati society, like other Arab countries, is very closed and exclusive, and sexuality or discussions of sexuality and sexual behaviour are definitely *haram.* In light of this it was embarrassing for her to admit that the number of street children in Dubai reached the many hundreds, products of illicit relationships between Emirati men and foreign women, usually workers from the Philippines or Malaysia. A raped woman is unclean; therefore, it's difficult for her to marry. One solution is that after the birth of an illegitimate child, the woman's family send her to a clinic to rebuild the hymen, thus "revirginating" the woman for marriage.

Abortion is not an option in any Middle Eastern country and certainly not in the Emirates, so when many of these street children are found, the Sheikh himself takes them in to one of his palaces and raises them as if they were his own. They obviously know he is not their father, but he gives each child a name, an identity, papers, education, cars, and money. The general public will never know their true identities. As they grow older, university education is provided so they can establish lives for themselves outside the Sheikh's paternal care. These children know who they are, but will never disclose the embarrassment of their birth to outsiders. It becomes a sort of pact between the children, the Sheikh, and the government to keep hidden the Emirati shame. But at least all of these children, whether in Senses[35] or under the Sheikh's protective umbrella, know the comfort of belonging, of receiving the best of care, living in clean surroundings, receiving an education, a way out, never witnessing or experiencing the utter despair of the Egyptian street children. In a country ruled by decrees the Emirates hide their shame under a Sheikh's protection.

When I showed Hanna these pictures, she cried. For her it was a double-edged sword. The Islahaya which she has devoted so much time and effort to fails to keep up all the work she does. She is also aware that

---

[35] *Senses* is the name of Nadia's Dubai Islahaya.

the Egyptian government refuses to recognize the plight of the girls, won't lift the proverbial finger to help them. They're incarcerated and what happens to them seems to be no concern of theirs.

Some may argue that there is an abundance of money in the Emirates as compared to Egypt. While this may be partially true, Nadia raises all her funds, for the teachers, food, education, and other necessities. The Sheikh contributes money for electricity and gave the land. In Egypt, the facilities are built, over the years Hanna and her committee have raised hundreds of thousands of pounds for upkeep which has only lasted a very short time as those in charge do not invest their time and energy to keep the facilities clean, nor do they teach the girls these basic skills.

Egypt does allocate enough money to raise the girls standard of living, what is really needed is more global public outcry at the kind of abuse the girls suffer,

have endured, and will endure unless the government

and people of Egypt decide to give these girls the

identity, education, and chance in life which all deserve.

Chapter Eight

Where Do We Go from Here?

Change is needed. It comes down to a desire to change, the desire to lift the stigma attached to the unfortunate girls forced to live on streets or in Islahayas. Concealed under the dirty cloak of government bureaucracy *Il Binait Dol* suffer from the harsh reality of isolation and ignorance. The street children of Egypt, visible as they roam city streets, are deliberately invisible to those who can make changes. Left to the devices of inefficient directors, disinterested officials, the system swallows them alive.

Amidst the political turmoil unsettling the Middle East at the moment, and the increased tension in Egypt putting a stranglehold on its people, the fate of these girls is at the bottom of the heap. No one has time to worry about the fate of street children, and no one really cares in fact reaction to them is often visibly violent and abusive. This is evident in one example; the recent CNN documentary *Girl Rising* considered the deep-seated educational needs of girls in developing countries. This is certainly true; however, in the documentary, the Egyptian story lacked honesty. Yasmin, the young heroine of the Egyptian segment was educated as evidenced by her knowledge of superhero comics. She also had a supportive mother who brought her to the police to report a rape by a rich Egyptian merchant. This was fantastic, as the reality is that women in Egypt do not willing go to police to report rapes. These violations are kept secret, girls often not even telling their mothers.

When the police officer called her a street girl, Yasmin's violent reaction against being called a street girl shows how the general public in Egypt views these homeless girls. Their stories should have been included in *Girl Rising* – not this fantastically created story of mother and daughter facing police questioning without fear. As a side note, the author of this segment admits that she has lost contact with the mother and daughter. Cairo in spite of its 20 million population has many of the qualities of a small village. Everyone knows everyone else, it's difficult to disappear – why and how did the author so easily lose contact with Yasmin and her mother?

Hiding the shame of street children serves no purpose. Egyptians have no time for the dark corners of Islahayas or their inmates; they are busy surviving themselves in political revolutions – hoping for change in their own lives. The government is failing its people, its people are failing its most vulnerable. Change must begin immediately. Egypt's future, its global reputation, and its place among world leaders are the stakes for which Egypt plays.

How to change attitudes is the question. Egyptian society views these girls in much the same light as the Untouchables of India appear to the general Indian population. They have little or no education or training, no families, which is paramount to Egyptians for general acceptability; without family, they have no name, no identity, and essentially no nationality. In some ways these girls are equivalent to the Bedoons living in the Emirates.[36] Neither are the street girls educated in their religion.

Adoption might be thought to provide another way out of their incarceration. In the West, adoption for

---

[36] These are people who have lived in the Emirates their entire lives, many born there, but since their families came from other countries, they have not been given Emirati citizenship; they exist in a virtual no-man's land, no country, no citizenship, no national benefits. The only difference between a Bedoon and an Egyptian street girl is that Bedoons possess passports from the country of their family origin.

those without parents is a possibility. Unfortunately,

for these girls, adoption is not a choice. Under Muslim

Shari'a law, the birth family is essential; without this, a

person remains without identity. In Islam, the family

name comes from the father, as does the child's religion

and heritage. Because of this adoption is not allowed.

If while living in the Islahaya they are fortunate

enough to obtain a basic education, even pass the

Adadaya exams, their options for self-sustenance

remain very limited. Their skills won't qualify them to

be shop assistants, they cannot continue their education

for the simple reason that they cannot leave the

Islahaya to attend a state school to obtain a high school

education, nor in the unlikely event they pass the high

school exams, university education is impossible. First,

their lack of identity precludes attending university;

lack of residence outside the Islahaya prohibits

attendance, and most importantly, lack of money for

fees, transportation, books, and other supplies, and basic living. The girls have only dreams of leaving the Islahaya; usually these dreams take the form of some prince charming coming to rescue them.

The roadblocks to the fulfilment of this dream of marriage are innumerable. First, if someone happens to ask for them in marriage, he must have enough money to pay for the marriage, pay for their living accommodations, and be prepared to support children. Second, as often happens, the mother-in-law moves in on the young couple, if not literally, then in everyday living. She becomes the voice to which the young wife must listen. The husband also listens to his mother, in disputes he often takes his mother's side, thus once more instilling his wife with a sense of isolation and rejection, continuing the cycle of disillusionment, and loss of self-respect. In the event the husband tires of her, or she hasn't fulfilled the child bearing requirement within the first year of marriage, the husband has the right to divorce her.

How do all these problems get changed or even addressed---one by one, without a steady stream of help, public awareness, and government concern. A former student, Sara, who worked with these girls, adds her initial reflections.

Amidst the crowded streets of Cairo, in a deeply congested area, is a large run-down building housing young girls who are, essentially, identity-less. Many of the girls living there do not have birth certificates, many of them are unrecognized by the state and have been cast aside, a problem of which very few are even aware, let alone concerned with.

I noticed, upon my first visit there, that the building was not far from where my hairdresser used to be. There was a hideous irony to this: in proximity to a place where so many young girls pass through on a daily

basis to have their hair done, nails manicured and egos

boosted, was a place where another sector of young girls,

in the same age group, lived with the sting of

abandonment and poverty. The proximity of these two

worlds only highlights just how unaware we all are–how

unaware I was of this world. Until the fall of 2006 when I

first visited, I had no idea that the building housing these

parent-less girls even existed.

I am not an easily shaken person, nor do I shy

away from possible awful situations. But, the

introductory visit my gender studies class made to the

Islahaya absolutely terrified me. Looking back now, I

think I was terrified for two reasons: first, because I

honestly was not sure if I had received all the necessary

vaccinations I might need considering the lack of

sanitation there, and second, because I did not know what

to expect of these young girls–would they become overly

friendly because of our visit? Or would they hate us for

having a better life?

Upon entering the building, its appearance was a

drab exterior which I expected, but the stench of cooking

oil was not. My dear friend and I, a girl who like me had

never before visited this kind of an institution, held hands

as we entered the building. Peeling wall plaster,

abandoned office space and the distant sounds of girls

squabbling is all I recall of that particular moment.

We were led up a flight of stairs and were told

that we were going to see where the girls slept, ate, and

had "classes"–then we were going to meet them. My

friend and I gripped onto one another as we walked up

the dim staircase. We heard a noise behind us, and as if

to pay homage to 1950s horror films, we gave one

another the 'I don't want to die today' looks as we stayed

at the back of the line of students going up the stairs. In

all honesty, we just didn't want to be the first ones in.

We were taken on a tour. We were shown the rooms where the girls slept. Mattresses were strewn over unclean floors and the rooms seemed over-crowded. There was little ventilation and the window glass was brown from dirt. I looked around to see the reactions of my fellow classmates--silence. None of us said a word except for one girl who made a distasteful remark about wanting to leave to go and have lunch somewhere. Following the gloomy bedrooms, we saw what was supposed to be a kitchen. I use the phrase "supposed to be" because it was not a kitchen; long, tired steel blocks made it look more like a morgue than a kitchen. The noises of excited and rowdy girls only grew louder and I felt myself becoming clammy and nervous. We entered a classroom and a large pool of smiling faces swarmed around us like bumblebees.

I wish I could say I instantly felt at ease and there were wondrous scenes of sympathy and humanity but it really wasn't like that. We were uncomfortable. The girls themselves were smiling–and after hearing some of their stories, horrible tales of rape, abandonment, being moved from one place to another, we decided we had to start smiling too, because frankly, we had no right not to.

I sat down beside another colleague as she spoke to a young girl with pretty eyes and messy hair. She was sweet, and intensely curious about my blonde hair and blue eyes. She shyly told my friend that she wanted to touch my hair so hers might one day resemble it, but she was afraid to. I asked her why she was afraid, and she answered that she might make it dirty. I felt sick; unhappy and ashamed to be carrying a handbag worth over three hundred US dollars.

We spent some time with the girls, listening to them, speaking with them. Of all the short speeches we heard, there is one that holds particular resonance for me; a young girl, sitting opposite me, explained to my friend and I that she had to learn how to read and write so she could work because she would never be able to marry someone and have a family. We asked her why she thought she would never marry, and she said, 'no one will marry a girl from here. They will never want us because we are less than everybody else.'[37]

The solutions themselves are simple: education, both practical self-help skills as in Dubai, and academic learning including useful trades, government concern, erasure of police records, and Islahaya directors who really understand the needs of these girls with the energy to implement real change. In addition to these basic changes, provide a clean, healthy, sanitary environment for the girls. Teach them how to care for their surroundings, give them daily chores rather than let the girls wander aimlessly behind locked gates for hours, days, month, and years on end. But the upshot is

---

[37] Contributed by my former student and Islahaya participant, Ms Sara el Masri.

that none of these changes will occur unless there is global and local awareness and positive action against the virtually sub-human existence forced on *Il Binait Dol, Those Girls.*

The outcome of the summer of June 2013 is uncertain. Regardless of the upshot of this last clash between the people and the Egyptian government, *Il Binait Dol*, those girls existing within the Islahayas will not see any relief in their circumstances. On the contrary, the demoralizing conditions in which they live does not change, it becomes worse. No one, least of all government and those with the power and authority to come to their aid, help; rather, they ignore those girls, treat them as they do the rubbish littering Cairo's streets. As so eloquently stated by one of the Islahaya girls, "*they will never want us because we are less than everybody else, we will never be one of them.*"

Author's Note

I never considered myself an activist. I have signed petitions, but I've never chained myself to an official's desk, never held banners or marched for various causes, although I do hold strong views about certain issues, in particular the role of women in society. Moving to Egypt changed my back bench approach to the problems women face, especially noticeable in Middle Eastern countries. The years I spent living in Egypt and other parts of the Middle East brought a certain problem to light, the situation of street children, or more specifically, street girls. With an estimate of between 50,000 and 200,000 homeless children wandering the streets of Cairo alone, one can only imagine how these children live. Of this huge number, an unknown number of girls, captured and labeled as criminals by the police, live in Islahayas, or in Arabic, places "to fix."

These fix-it places supposedly give the girls homes, education, and protection. However, the reality doesn't come close to the idea. They live in virtual prisons, in filthy conditions, eating food that may or may not be fresh. They are the forgotten of Egyptian society. They have no voice, no hope of normalcy, plenty of dreams, with virtually no chance of fulfillment. Growing up, I knew the terror of no voice, silenced at every turn. It is the same for these girls, so writing this book is a way to give them a collective voice. Speaking up for these girls is a dangerous business in Egypt. In the eyes of the law, they are criminals, no matter their ages, no matter the circumstances which led them to street life.

In 2011, shortly after the first Arab Spring, I began writing about my experiences with these girls. Since that time, much has happened politically and is still ongoing with no immediate solution in sight.

Waiting in the women's queue to enter the Square – January 2011

This book, *Il Binait Dol, Egypt's Hidden Shame,* is dedicated in two parts, one to the street girls who only want to become part of society, heard, accepted, needed, and understood and who deserve a voice, deserve a way out; second to Hanna Hartmann-Hosni, the woman who virtually single-handed has championed these girls for nearly twenty years. The world reads about the starving children of Darfur, we know about the horrors of sex trade involving young girls from many countries, we admire celebrities who devote their wealth and time to these causes. But these street girls, *Il Binait Dol,* incarcerated and without identities within the Islahayas, escape global view. Egypt's government hides these girls, it's their hidden shame; those in power want no one to be aware. But it is time to bring *Il Binait Dol* out of Egypt's shadows to world attention, particularly now, when Egypt is attempting to convince the global community that democracy for all Egyptians is a focal part of its political agenda.

Since 2011 political events and more revolution continues to upset the delicate political situation in Egypt. The first revolution, the Arab Spring of 25

January 2011 gave the Egyptian people a taste for change, for a voice which they'd never had.

Voices of the people – Tahrir Square January 2011

Dissatisfied with the initial results of the 2011 Arab Spring, a substantial majority of Egyptians rose up once again, and created the atmosphere for another political upheaval which occurred on 30 June 2013. The Egyptian people chose that those who died in 2011 would not have done so in vain.

Commemorating some who died in the January 2011 Revolution

They ousted Mohamed Morsi and the Muslim

Brotherhood from office replacing them with an interim

government headed by Adli Mansour, the interim

president alongside General Abdul-Fattah el-Sisi,

Egypt's military head. Others in the new interim cabinet include Mohamed el Baradei[38] and Hazem el-Beblawi, the interim prime minister.

While these men attempt to reorganize Egypt into a government acceptable to the people, opposition demonstrations organized by the Muslim Brotherhood continue. In the midst of this turmoil the girls locked away in the Islahayas throughout Egypt cannot even give voice to the insidious environment in which they are forced to live. This is my activism, to help give the attention, voice, and help which is given to so many others throughout the world to *Il Binait Dol, Egypt's Hidden Shame.*

---

[38] Unfortunately, Mr Baradei just resigned (August 2013) giving as his reason that his desire for peaceful negotiations rather than the ongoing violence were being ignored. He could not support the extensive killings incurred since the deposition of Mr Morsi.

Acknowledgments

My initial interest in the street children of Egypt came when I was an assistant professor of history at the American University in Cairo. Teaching a gender history course, I recognized the need to bring my students from the theory of textbooks to the reality of gender disparity in Egypt. After initial trepidation at being exposed to the horrific conditions in which *Il Binait Dol* (in Arabic *Those Girls*) lived, the students engaged wholeheartedly with these unfortunate children.

My first acknowledgment goes to Il Binait Dol, Egypt's street girls, whose lives and tragedies comprise the content of this book. Their stories deserve as much publicity as possible in this twenty-first century. Just like the starving children and human tragedies in other parts of the world, these girls and the human heartbreak through which they exist, is worth the time and telling.

I owe a virtually unrepayable debt to the dedication and hard work of Hanna Hartmann-Hosni and to her greatest supporter, her husband Souhail Hosni. Without their tireless efforts on behalf of Egypt's Il Binait Dol, I would never have become aware of this particular shame in Egypt. Next, my students, whose dedication to the course projects and the girls (and boys) of Egypt's Islahayas gratified all those who saw the importance of this type of commitment by students. At the American University in Cairo, Professor Ann Lesch (vice-provost, retired) lent her willing support to this course. She immediately appreciated the significance of using this course and the students' enthusiasm as one of the pioneering community-based courses endorsed by the university. Professor Lesch's extensive experience and expertise in the Middle East is reflected in her dedication to this as well as many other important projects relating to the Middle East. The University was also very supportive and rewarded me with a teaching exemplar award for this course for which I was surprised and very grateful for their acknowledgement of its importance.

I am further indebted to Frances Jones-Davies, editor and owner of Cambria magazine in Wales. Without her encouragement to write these stories, and the provision of a wonderful Welsh cottage for a few weeks one idyllic summer, they might still be in a bin somewhere waiting to be told. Also I give thanks to Jinnie and Derek Goodlake who offered me their home, hospitality, friendship, and sound advice while I worked on this task. My good friend and partner in business, Lynn Kordus who has stuck through this project, reading a very rough first draft, working with me, and especially offering thoughtful editorial support to bring this book to fruition, deserves appreciative thanks.

Many more friends and family can be listed here, two in particular, my dear friends Nancy Sellars and Cara whose positive reflections and words of encouragement kept the creative light burning. Without their nudges across the continents I may not have had the courage to complete this book. I cannot end these acknowledgements without expressing my indebtedness to my Egyptian friend and colleague, Nevien Samir. Without her assistance in talking to the girls, getting them to confide in her, partly because she spoke to them in Arabic, partly she related to the girls as a young Egyptian woman and they felt safe to confide their stories, and mostly her unfailing friendship and continuing loyalty throughout this project from its earliest inception.

Further Reading

Below is a short list of website links to articles about the current conditions in Egypt. There are no readings about *Il Binait Dol* simply because no one has cared enough to investigate and write about the situation facing these girls.

Egypt Unravels – June 2013:
http://www.foreignaffairs.com/articles/139541/mara-revkin/the-egyptian-state-unravels

Revealed: 100 Most Powerful Arab Women 2013
http://www.arabianbusiness.com/revealed-100-most-powerful-arab-women-2013-491648.html

Egypt "bodyguards" take stand against sex assault
By BRIAN ROHAN | Associated Press – Sat, Feb 2, 2013
http://www.huffingtonpost.com/2013/02/02/egypt-sexual-assault_n_2605683.html

Fatwa issued on baby Burkas
http://english.alarabiya.net/articles/2013/02/03/264031.html

INSIGHT: Women of the Arab Spring, Beyond Objects and Subjects
January 29, 2013, by Natana J. DeLong-Bas
http://middleeastvoices.voanews.com/author/natana-j-delong-bas/

Arab Spring to take years to improve women's rights-activists by Belinda Goldsmith Reuters/Tuesday 4 December 2012
http://www.reuters.com/article/2012/12/04/us-women-arabspring-idUSBRE8B314F20121204

What the Arab Spring has done for women's equality, in one chart
Posted by Max Fisher on October 25, 2012, at 4:30 pm
http://www.washingtonpost.com/blogs/worldviews/wp/2012/10/25/what-the-arab-spring-has-done-for-womens-equality-in-one-chart/

The Arab Spring: Changing the Lives of Women in the Middle East and North Africa by Khadija Safi-Eddine/ Morocco World News, May 4, 2012
http://www.moroccoworldnews.com/2012/03/32938/the-arab-spring-changing-the-lives-of-women-in-the-middle-east-and-north-africa/

Read more at Middle East Voices:
http://middleeastvoices.voanews.com/2013/01/insight-women-of-the-arab-spring-beyond-objects-and-subjects-70868/

Reflections on Women in the Arab Spring: In Celebration of International Women's Day 2012: Women's Voices from Around the World. Middle East Program Woodrow Wilson Center for Scholars, eds. Kendra Heideman and Mona Youssef
http://www.wilsoncenter.org/article/reflections-women-the-arab-spring-women%E2%80%99s-voices-around-the-world

The links below discuss the most recent political events as of August 2013, as the days progress into weeks and months, more articles will appear – it is essential to search out information which gives insight into all sides of the current political dilemma facing Egypt and Egyptians. To that end it is suggested that interested readers pay close attention to the website and writings of Mr Ismail Serageldin, director of the Alexandria Library in Alexandria, Egypt.

https://www.facebook.com/photo.php?v=1020142880
0577064

http://www.raymondibrahim.com/from-the-arab-
world/inside-egypts-terrorist-camps-torture-rape-
mass-murder/

http://www.serageldin.com/NewsDetails.aspx?NewsID
=BKd7g2ROyrNz2w3b8Suo6w%3d%3d